MARKETING MADE SIMPLE

MARKETING MADE SIMPLE

A STEP-BY-STEP STORYBRAND
GUIDE FOR ANY BUSINESS

DONALD MILLER

WITH DR. J. J. PETERSON

HARPERCOLLINS
LEADERSHIP

AN IMPRINT OF HARPERCOLLINS

Published by HarperCollins Leadership, an imprint of HarperCollins Focus LLC.

Book design by Aubrey Khan, Neuwirth & Associates.

ISBN 978-1-4002-0380-2 (eBook)
ISBN 978-1-4002-0379-6 (HC)

Library of Congress Control Number: 2020930312

Printed in the United States of America
20 21 22 23 LSC 10 9 8 7 6 5 4 3 2 1

CONTENTS

CONTENTS

INTRODUCTION

Marketing should be easy and it should work.

Whether you run a small business or a large business, the easiest and best marketing plan starts with a sales funnel.

It doesn't matter what you sell, if you use words to sell your products, a sales funnel will work.

A sales funnel is the basic foundation of a good digital marketing plan. Once you create a sales funnel, your advertising can then support your sales funnel.

While there is more to marketing than a digital plan, your digital strategy, including your website, lead generator, and email campaign will serve as the foundation for all your other collateral.

But, most importantly, you need a sales funnel—and this book will teach you to create one.

A sales funnel is a way to capture and convert leads.

Every entrepreneur, business owner, and marketer must know how a sales funnel works. Whether you create a sales funnel yourself or have somebody else create it for you, the checklist in this book will spell out everything you need to know to build a sales funnel that works. Each chapter of this book will give you tips and strategies for creating each piece correctly.

At MarketingMadeSimple.com you can download a free paper wireframe that, along with this book, will save you an enormous amount of time and mental anguish.

At StoryBrand, we've helped over ten thousand small, medium, and large size companies create sales funnels that work. Nearly all of them started by simply filling out these pieces of paper.

When you download your paper wireframe, you'll also get two sample wireframes to help you understand where you are headed.

This book is all about making the execution of a marketing strategy easy. We can talk about marketing all day, but you will only make money on what you execute.

Most marketing plans do not fail in intent or philosophy of communication, they fail in execution. People simply don't get it done.

Last year, my contributing writer Dr. J. J. Peterson turned in his doctoral dissertation on the StoryBrand messaging framework. In the dissertation J. J. defended the idea that the framework works for any kind of business, large or small, B2B or B2C. However, J. J. found that success with the framework hinges on one crucial imperative: execution. This book is all about execution. It exists to help you get the job done.

If you have a clear message and no sales funnel, your business will not grow. Your visitors will assume you can't solve their problem and they will leave in search of someone who can.

DON'T WASTE YOUR MONEY ON MARKETING THAT DOESN'T WORK

If you haven't started spending money on marketing yet, this book will save you thousands if not millions of dollars. And if you've been wasting money on marketing, this book will stop that waste in its tracks.

Over the years we've run StoryBrand, we've met lots of marketing agencies that will sell you new logos, color schemes, and brand guidelines followed by Facebook ads and slick landing pages. Without a sales funnel in place, most of that stuff won't work.

J. J. and I have trained hundreds of StoryBrand certified marketing guides and in that time experimented with dozens of marketing ideas. Yet we keep coming back to the old, trusty sales funnel.

The checklist in this book will get results.

If you are an entrepreneur, a business owner, or serve in the marketing department of a large organization, this book will serve as an easy-to-understand blueprint.

If you're in charge of the marketing for your company, consider this your new playbook. And if you run a company, hand this book to your marketing team and ask them to create exactly what is in this checklist.

PAYING FOR MARKETING THAT DOESN'T WORK IS WRONG

It is wrong for a marketing company to charge you money and fail to get you a return on your investment. It's an equal injustice that you, personally, would spend your time on an effort that does not pay you for your work. Your time is too valuable for that.

If you read this book and need help, visit MarketingMadeSimple.com where you can find a StoryBrand certified guide to create your sales funnel for you. Even if you hire a guide, however, this book will be important to show you what the guide will be doing. You will be able to offer valuable direction and feedback in the creation of your marketing plan after you fully understand what your marketing plan should be.

Marketing does not have to be complicated. Do what we've laid out in this book and you'll have confidence in your marketing, you'll grow your mission, and you will connect with customers.

Let's get started.

Part I

THE THREE STAGES
OF RELATIONSHIP

1

THE ONE MARKETING PLAN YOU WILL NEVER REGRET

Twenty years ago I'd just written my first bestselling book. I'd written a book before that but my mother was the only one who bought copies, so that doesn't count. It took me two tries to write a book people actually wanted to read, and from what I hear, even hitting it big on your second try is pretty rare. More than 99 percent of book writers fail to sell enough copies to make a living. I was lucky.

After writing a bestselling book, I thought, everything else would come easy. I assumed every book I'd release after that would also be a bestseller. I assumed thousands of people would show up every time I gave a speech. And I supposed I could make movies out of my books and become some kind of literary/Hollywood phenomenon.

It turns out that for more than 99 percent of writers who write a bestselling book, none of that other stuff happens.

Writing a bestseller is a huge help, but thousands of bestselling authors have dwindled away their money and influence so that, in the end, they had nothing to show for it. And that's what nearly happened to me.

Instead of building a platform, I rested on my past success. In my calculation, I wasted about ten years not taking my opportunity as a successful author (and human being) seriously.

If I could go back in time twenty years, this book is the letter I'd write to myself.

I know it sounds strange to say if I could go back twenty years I'd sit down and teach myself a basic marketing plan, but it's true.

Not having a marketing plan cost me millions of dollars, serious international influence, and the chance to accomplish at least some of my dreams.

Don't get me wrong. Things have turned out okay, but the only reason things worked out is because I executed this plan.

THE FIVE-STEP MARKETING PLAN THAT WORKS

In short, there are five things I should have done twenty years ago to keep the momentum going. And after I did these five things, I should have done them again and then again and then again.

They are ridiculously pragmatic. Here they are:

1. **Created a BrandScript.** I should have clarified my message.
2. **Created a one-liner.** I should have distilled that message into a single sentence.
3. **Wireframed a landing page.** I should have elaborated on that message and brought it to life on a clear and compelling website.
4. **Created a lead-generating PDF.** I should have used a lead generator to capture emails.

5. **Created an email campaign.** I should have earned the trust of people who had given me their email address by sending them helpful emails that practically solved their problems.

This is a book about building a platform and growing a company. I'm going to keep it simple and specific.

Most business books are long on theory and short on application, but J. J. and I are going to tell you exactly what you should do and what order you should do it in so that your marketing works.

THIS PLAN WILL DIG YOU OUT OF A HOLE

I learned to execute this simple marketing plan because I had to.

Twenty years ago, after having sold millions of books, I lost everything.

I put all my money into an investment that failed.

On a bright and cool September morning I got a call saying the investment hadn't worked and that my life savings was gone.

It was one of the hardest seasons of my life. I felt like I'd squandered everything.

In the weeks following that excruciating loss, I realized I'd not taken responsibility for my career. I'd trusted outside managers, publicists, investors, and publishers to guide me.

I decided then to become the CEO of my own life. I'd make the decisions.

I rebuilt.

Instead of writing another book, sending it to the publisher, and hoping for another bestseller, I self-published my next book and started a little company. I began searching for an inexpensive marketing plan that would work, and after years of experimenting, came up with the plan that is in this book.

Today, my wife and I own a company called Business Made Simple that is tackling the problem of college debt by offering inexpensive online business courses to anybody trying to develop themselves.

Today, only seven years later, we give away more to charity every year than I lost on that Monday morning.

How did all this happen? Following this simple, five-step marketing plan over and over is what built my company and rebuilt my life.

The good news is, you don't have to lose all your money to build a great company. If you follow the five steps outlined in this book, you'll grow your brand correctly the first time.

If you work for a large company, this plan will work for every division and every product within each division. Yes, you can use this book to create multiple sales funnels. In fact, I recommend doing exactly that. Once you create your first sales funnel, start working on the next one. Ultimately, your marketing plan will exist of many sales funnels, each selling your products and services to varying demographics.

Regardless of whether you're a small company creating a few sales funnels or a large company creating hundreds, the plan works.

You do not have to struggle with marketing. You can be confident, proud, and see a return.

If you execute the plan that is in this book, you will succeed.

2

THE ACTUAL STAGES OF A RELATIONSHIP

Why People Have to Get Curious and Enlightened Before They Will Commit

Our five-step marketing plan will invite people into a trusted relationship with your brand. Not only will you sell more products, but customers will start thinking of you, your salespeople, and even your products as friends who are helping them on their journey.

Understanding the stages of a relationship is important because it helps us understand what our sales funnel has to accomplish.

We all want people to understand how our products can solve their problems so that they will make a purchase. But it turns out, simply asking people to buy our products doesn't work. At least not right away.

Asking for a sale is a relational proposition. And relationships have rules.

Most of us ask people to buy our products the way a shy, young boy might ask a girl to go on a date. We clumsily walk up to her in the hallway, shake her hand with a strong grip the way our dad taught us, and ask her if she'd like to go to a movie with us and our mom, who just bought a new car. (I'm relating the story for a friend.)

Who knows whether that relationship will work out. Let's hope so for the kid's sake. Regardless, though, the kid would do a lot better if he understood how relationships really work. And the truth is relationships are built slowly.

Whether we are talking about a romantic relationship, a friendship, or even a relationship with a brand, all relationships move through three stages. And, these stages cannot be rushed.

The stages of a relationship are:

1. Curiosity
2. Enlightenment
3. Commitment

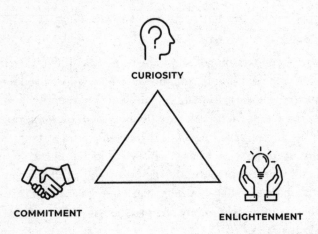

People do not want to be enlightened about you (get to know you more) unless they are curious about you (you have something that can help them survive), and until they are enlightened about how you can help them survive, they will never commit.

Every relationship you have ever been in has gone through these three stages. Even relationships you have with brands.

THE JOURNEY EVERY CUSTOMER TAKES

Recently I began exploring high-end audio equipment. Betsy and I live in Nashville and because so many people in this town are in the music industry, we often find ourselves hosting small get-togethers with artists who are working on an album.

After the fifth or sixth impromptu listening party, I realized the tiny Bluetooth speaker in our kitchen wasn't good enough.

I spent a little time on Google and came across a small company named Oswalds Mill Audio that makes custom audio equipment. The pictures of the speakers and turntables were beautiful. The turntable itself weighed eighty pounds and the speakers looked like steel bullhorns pulled from an old football stadium. Everything was mounted on beautiful hardwood, and the guy in the picture playing the vinyl record was wearing a cool sweater, which is the sign of a guy who knows a lot about how a sound system works. Anyway, there was something different about this sound system and the way the product was talked about on the website that made me curious.

But how? And curious about what?

I'll tell you whether I bought the sound system in a minute, but first, let's explore what we need to do to help a customer be more interested in a brand.

Stage 1: Curiosity

Can this person, product, or service help me survive? The first stage of a relationship is curiosity. This is the stage where you meet somebody and you want to know more about them. At a party, this is the person you leave the party hoping for a second interaction with. Perhaps you went to the same school or perhaps they are a few years ahead of you in the same career.

Without knowing it, what's making you curious about this person is one thing: you sense they can help you survive or thrive.

You might wonder how a person can help you survive just by having gone to the same school as you. The truth is, the filter that decides what helps us survive is incredibly nuanced and particular. Your filter is a ridiculously refined instrument.

That person who went to the same school as you solves the problem of you not feeling alone, that there is somebody who has a similar life journey as yours. We tend to collect people with similar life journeys for that very reason; they make us feel like we have a tribe.

Being alone, by the way, is a vulnerable state. Human beings move in families and tribes. We may go through seasons where we are alone but mostly we like being around other human beings.

When we meet somebody who is like us, we feel more safe, mainly because we understand the person better. Confusion about who somebody is makes us feel slightly threatened, so similarities break down those threats faster.

If the person we are talking to is a few years ahead of us in the same career, the way they can help us survive is more obvious. They can help us avoid pitfalls and may know some strategies so our career can advance a little faster.

None of this thinking is happening on a conscious level, of course, but it's definitely happening.

A person, product, or brand that can help us survive or thrive activates a survival mechanism within us that piques our curiosity.

Curiosity Is a Snap Judgment
The curiosity stage of a relationship is mostly about snap judgments. Scanning our environment is like sorting through a stack of mail.

We place anything we see as junk, or not relevant to our survival, in the recycle bin. Bills, letters from friends, catalogs we might be interested in, and such go into a pile to be sorted later. At the curiosity stage we are really only making two large piles: *keep* and *discard*.

This is how our customers' brains work as they scan the three thousand pieces of marketing collateral they encounter each day. The overwhelming majority of material gets discarded, but the occasional message gets sorted to the keep pile.

I know this all sounds harshly utilitarian, but it's quite normal and healthy. Each of us are trying to live a meaningful story, and not everybody or everything is useful to whatever story we've decided to live.

Human beings collect physical, emotional, and social resources that help them survive in the world. Just like the squirrels in my backyard collect nuts, we collect anything we might need to stay alive on this planet. And that's not a bad thing. We are, after all, primates. And primates are terrific at survival.

A person with no curiosity filter would not survive in the world. In fact, people with no curiosity filter wouldn't even make it out of their house in the morning. They'd just stand in the kitchen all day wondering about how the toaster works. Why? Because their curiosity filter wouldn't tell them they don't need to know how the toaster works and that if they don't leave soon they will be late to work and if that keeps happening they will lose their job.

The point is this: if you don't tell somebody how you can help them survive, they will set you aside—or worse, discard you.

When it comes to marketing, the header on your website, the subject line of your email, the opening statement of your proposal, the title of your lead generator, your entire elevator pitch, the first line of your keynote address, and a thousand other things need to succinctly express one of the ways you help people survive. If they don't, people will not listen.

How Do You Get Past a Person's Curiosity Filter?

So what made me curious about the expensive audio equipment? Several things, most of which were being communicated to my subconscious.

The main thing that made me curious was status. More than even a sound system that sounded good, the beautiful equipment was going to make my living room look and feel awesome. People were going to think more of me when they saw that equipment (or so my primate mind believed), and so the pictures on the website were doing a lot of the heavy lifting. Not only that, but the guy in the sweater was acting as a proxy for my aspirational identity. Who wouldn't want to be ten years younger dressed in a cool sweater listening to an Al Green record while their spouse mixed them an old-fashioned in the background? Fantastic!

I know it all sounds irrational, but very little of what makes us curious is actually rational. People don't buy products, vote for candidates, or join a movement because they are thinking rationally. If you look around, that's pretty obvious.

Regardless, the point is this: to pique somebody's curiosity, you must associate your products with something that will help them survive.

Your Customers Are Not Curious About You, They Are Curious About How You Can Solve Their Problem

Most businesses make the enormous mistake of telling their story to their customers, as though their customers are somehow interested. Customers are not interested in your story. They are, rather, interested in being invited into a story that has them surviving and winning in the end.

Instead of telling your story, the first stage of your marketing plan should pique a customer's curiosity about how their own story could be made better.

Curiosity Isn't Enough

Curiosity aside, I still wasn't ready to buy the expensive sound system. The sound system was no impulse buy. I needed more information.

Without knowing it, I was moving into the second stage of relationships. I wanted the company to enlighten me about how, exactly, their product was going to increase my chances of survival.

Stage 2: Enlightenment

This is the process by which your customer begins to trust you. If curiosity is what gets us to pay attention to a brand, enlightenment invites us into a relationship.

I'm not talking about the "you'll understand the meaning of the universe" kind of enlightenment: I'm talking about the kind of enlightenment that helps us understand how something works.

An enlightened person is somebody who understands and an unenlightened person is somebody who doesn't. You are either enlightened about how the tectonic plates once moved, or you are not. And that goes for physics, gardening, neuroscience, or how to make snow cones. With the exception of how to actually eat snow cones, I, for example, am not enlightened about any of those things.

If you want customers to take the next step in a relationship with your brand, you need to enlighten them about how you can solve their problem and help them survive.

After piquing your customers' curiosity on a website, in an email, or in some form of advertising or sales presentation, the next question they will likely ask is "but how?"

You sell a medicine that can cure a hangover. But how does it work?

You can improve education without raising taxes. But how?

You can safely rid their garden of pesky pests. But how?

The next phase of your marketing should enlighten them about how your products work to solve their problems.

Notice I didn't say that you should enlighten your customers about how your product works. That's hardly important. You should enlighten your customers about how your product *works to solve their problem.*

Never forget, we are not telling our story or even talking about our products. We are always inviting our customers on a journey in which their lives are made better through the use of our products.

Customers being invited on a journey want to know what tools we have to help them save the day and exactly how those tools will help them accomplish whatever task lays before them. If they are confused about how our products can help them win, they will walk away without making a purchase.

Customers Will Not Move Into a Fog

Being confused about something is a vulnerable state. If you drive a car in a country where traffic rules are different, your confusion could get you hurt. If you are confused about what kind of berries are poisonous and what kind are edible, you could get killed!

A human brain is designed to experience pleasure when it understands something and fear or resistance when it doesn't. This is a basic survival mechanism and it's one that very few companies take into account when they communicate with their customers.

When somebody is confused, in varying degrees, they feel exposed to danger. Therefore, people move away from situations in which they are confused and toward contexts in which they understand the situation and feel in control.

This principle is why politicians with repeatable, simple messaging statements usually win. It's not because their plan will work or has even been thought through, it's because voters feel a sense of understanding and associate that feeling of comfort and survival with that candidate.

The answer to confusion is always no.

When you enlighten your customers, you lift the fog and help them see clearly how your product can help them solve their problem.

If the header of your website, the first words of your proposal, or even the first thing you say in a keynote is meant to pique curiosity, the next idea you communicate should answer the "but how."

Your Marketing Should Enlighten Customers

I built StoryBrand, the marketing division of BusinessMadeSimple, using a lead-generating PDF called "Five Things Your Website Should Include" because my potential customers wanted to know more. I convinced them their message wasn't clear enough and then taught them how to clarify their message in a specific application. That lead generator was incredibly successful for me. It was a great "next step" in my customers' relational journey with my brand.

There are many ways you can enlighten your customers, including long-form copy toward the bottom of your website in a lead generator, a live event, an email sequence, or even a video.

As I did further research on the speaker company, I found a video in which the founder explained how sound waves work. It turns out sound waves take up actual physical space. Some sound waves are an inch wide, and others are two or three inches wide. What this means is if you have speakers that aren't the right dimensions to produce the physical sound waves, those waves become distorted.

The video enlightened me. No wonder the cheap Bluetooth speaker in our kitchen was so inferior. My speaker was squishing the precious sound waves!

After becoming enlightened, I realized *why* the sound coming from these new expensive speakers would deliver a terrific experience. And, of course, I wanted the experience all the more.

One thing the video could have done a little better would have been to connect the enlightenment about how their speakers work with my own survival. A simple line saying "so that's why your friends aren't super impressed with your current sound system and they will be really impressed when you install ours" would sell a lot more speakers. Why? Because now your big bullhorn speakers don't just help me listen to music, they help me bond with and serve my tribe.

As you think about your marketing campaigns, are you piquing your customers' curiosity and then enlightening them as to how you can solve their problems, help them survive, and improve their lives?

Later in this book we will give you step-by-step instructions on how to do this, but for now, know that even these first two steps are not enough. Now that we are in a trusted relationship with our customers, we have to ask them to commit.

Stage 3: Commitment

The point at which your customer is asked to make a risky decision. The two main reasons customers do not place orders are because:

1. The brand never asked them for the sale, or
2. The brand asked them for a sale too early.

The reason asking for a commitment too early in a relationship doesn't work is because a commitment is risky, and taking risks works against our survival mechanisms.

Making our customers curious and then gradually enlightening them reduces the sense of risk and greatly increases the chance they will commit their hard-earned dollars on our products.

Timing Is Everything

The day I met my wife I knew I wanted to marry her. I did. Much later, of course. But the morning we met, it was all I could do to patiently wait and take small steps.

I was in and out of D.C. working on a government task force, and she worked at a bed and breakfast I was staying at. My only goal the morning we first met was to not spill coffee on my shirt as we sat at the breakfast table and talked. Luckily, I made it through that breakfast alive and could tell she was open to another conversation in the future.

But that's when I screwed up. As we e-mailed back and forth over the next month, I never made my intentions known. Because I wasn't asking her out, she assumed I only wanted to be friends and started dating somebody else. It would be nearly three more years before I had the chance to recover from my mistake.

What I should have said early on was that I enjoyed talking to her and whenever I happened to be in D.C. next, I'd love to take her on a date. If I'd have just said that, I might have gotten an earlier start on a great love story.

The reason I didn't ask her out, though, was the same reason many of us don't ask our customers to commit. We are a little scared of rejection and we don't want to come off as pushy.

When the time is right, though, we have to make our intentions known or we will lose the relationship.

We often believe that being passive is a way of respecting our customer. We don't ask for the sale because we don't want them to be bothered. However, the last thing we want our customers saying is something along the lines of "I really like that brand, I consider them a friend, but I don't buy anything from them. I do, however, make out with their competitor all the time."

Blah.

Wise men say only fools rush in, but wise men also make a move eventually.

Move Slow, But Move

Having a "buy now" button on your website is not pushy. Customers always want to know where the relationship is going and you want to make sure to tell them that this relationship is a business relationship that is transactional in nature. They will respect you for being honest. Having a "buy now" or "schedule a call" button on your website makes sure they always understand the kind of relationship you are inviting them into.

Businesses that pretend to be their customers' friend in order to create sales come off as users and stalkers. As a business leader, it's our role to be trusted advisors to our customers. And customers absolutely love trusted advisors. We do not have to take the place of their parents or their spouses. That's creepy.

Later in the book when we teach you to wireframe a website, we'll show you how to always be asking for the sale without being pushy.

And being pushy is a problem.

When a sales relationship moves too quickly, the customer feels threatened. The reason people feel threatened is because making a purchase is always a decision to forgo valuable survival resources in exchange for resources they hope will increase their chances of survival even more. If they are wrong in that calculation, they are under greater threat than they were before they made the purchase.

That's why so many people hate it when a car salesman rushes out of the building when we walk onto a lot to shop for a car. Nobody wants to be "tricked" into giving up their resources. They want to be invited into a journey in which they will discover a product that can help them survive, and preferably for a great value.

The same is true in social relationships. Commitment in a relationship takes time.

Why does commitment take time? Because commitment is the first stage in a relationship in which a person has to take a calculated risk. Commitment is when they put skin in the game.

Rushed Relationships Are Not Healthy

We all remember how relationships felt in junior high. We'd have a best friend one week and a new one the following week. We fell in love one month only to fall in love with somebody else a month later. As we grew older, the pace of those transitions slowed down and became healthier.

If an adult falls in love with somebody new every couple months, most people would think of that person as unhealthy and not want to risk being with them.

I say that because when we rush in to close a deal or make a sale too soon, the customer smells "unhealth."

Our sales funnels should invite people into a journey that never attempts to trick or coerce them to make a decision they will later regret. That's one of the keys to staying in business for decades rather than months.

When we push customers to make a purchase, we end up with frustrated customers—or worse, unhealthy customers who don't have good boundaries. The latter tend to light up our customer service lines and create more problems than the sale was worth.

It's true you always want to be asking for the sale, but if the relationship is moving at the right pace asking for the sale, even when the customer isn't ready, won't break the deal. Always piquing their curiosity while enlightening them allows a customer to reject your offer while still asking to know more.

The key to marketing—and sales for that matter—is to invite the customer on a journey at the pace of a natural, healthy relationship.

To Create a Good Relationship You Must Keep in Touch

So what's the correct pace? In my opinion, for most products a customer needs to experience about eight touchpoints before they are ready to place an order.

A "touch" in this context is an email, a visit to your website, a radio ad, a keynote that they hear, or any other piece of marketing collateral you send their way.

The sad news is, in order for your touchpoints to reach a customer eight times, you need to send out dozens of pieces of communication they may actually ignore. In other words, you may have to reach out to them fifty times just to get your customer to notice.

The less expensive the product, the more likely they are to impulse buy, which means fewer touches. But the more expensive the product, the more they will need to hear from you before they will take a risk.

The absolute best way to stay in a relationship with a customer is to email them. Depending on the kind of email campaign you are creating, you will continue piquing their curiosity, further enlighten them, and call them to action.

In the email section of this book, we will help you craft emails that do all three. Of specific importance to you, though, are the emails that close the deal.

Customers can be invited on a journey that builds a trusting relationship and invites them to buy your products all through email.

You should have an email campaign for every product you sell. Likely your salespeople should be interacting with clients at various stages of an email campaign.

A Sales Funnel Controls the Pace of the Relationship

In a relationship, you talk about things on a fourth or fifth date you might never talk about on a first date. Intimacy and trust take time.

The rest of this book will walk you through the creation of a sales funnel that will build trust with your customers in a way that is natural and safe.

As you create your sales funnel, you will be piquing your customers' curiosity, enlightening them, and then asking them to commit. Different pieces of your sales funnel will accomplish these tasks and to some degree they overlap, but in the end your customer will enjoy interacting with your brand because you've respected their autonomy and space.

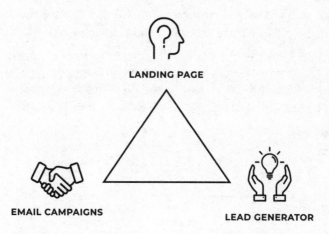

LANDING PAGE

EMAIL CAMPAIGNS

LEAD GENERATOR

Assess the Strength of Your Marketing Campaign

Are you piquing your customers' curiosity with your website, your signage, the first pages of your proposals, and through the talking points your salespeople employ?

Are you earning your customers' trust by enlightening them about how you can solve their problems and help them survive?

Are you inviting your customers to place an order through a complimentary and direct ask?

Once you create your sales funnel, you'll be inviting your customers into a trusted relationship that feels safe, consistent, and useful in their lives.

People fall in love with brands for the same reason they fall in love with each other. The brand helped them survive and got them a great return on their social, emotional, or financial investment.

What if a significant amount of trust building could be automated? What if, by the time you or one of your sales representatives sat down with a potential client, it felt like that client was already on the fourth or fifth date with your brand?

How much would your sales increase if by the time you interacted with a potential customer your customer's curiosity had already been piqued and your brand had enlightened them on how you could solve their problem?

Customers can fall in love with your brand too. Just invite them into the stages of a relationship and do so at the right pace.

The Marketing Made Simple Checklist will show you the way.

3

AN INTRODUCTION TO THE MARKETING MADE SIMPLE CHECKLIST

Many companies confuse branding with marketing, and this confusion is costing them millions.

Branding affects how a customer feels about your brand, while marketing communicates a specific offer.

Branding concerns itself with fonts and colors and design, while marketing puts the right words together to pique a customer's interest and close the deal.

Most of us are so concerned with the way our brand looks and feels, we neglect to communicate what customers are actually looking for: a solution to their problem.

Imagine getting a job as an NFL football coach and spending 90 percent of your time choosing the new team logo, the new jersey designs, and the "branding" for game-day trinkets the team will hand out to fans? Meanwhile, your team hasn't been drilled on the fundamentals of the game.

It doesn't matter how pretty your jerseys are, your team is going to lose.

It's easy for us to think of branding as more important than marketing. We watch the Super Bowl and get sentimental when the new Coca-Cola commercial comes on. We want people to feel just as great about our company. What we fail to realize is that Coca-Cola is a household brand name. Coke was invented in the nineteenth century and brilliantly marketed in the early twentieth century. Hundreds of millions of dollars have been spent telling the world what Coca-Cola is. And not only this, we've all tasted it and enjoyed it. Coke has extreme brand familiarity, which means they can afford do to more branding and less marketing.

Now imagine a company that has created an automotive product allowing you to only change the oil in your car once every year. That would be a pretty amazing product. Let's say you can drive up to fifteen thousand miles between oil changes. Incredible. The problem is, nobody has heard of this company. A rookie mistake would be to "brand" the company rather than "market" the product.

A novice marketing director might want to use a tag line like "save time, save money," which at first glance sounds great. But look again. To an outsider, it's invisible language. Let's say you're driving down the street and see a random company logo on a billboard with giant words that say "save time, save money." If you didn't know what the product did or what problem the product solved, would that mean anything to you? No! People don't pull their cars over to sit on their hood and study billboards. They pass by them at eighty miles per hour. That billboard needs to say "The oil you only have to change once a year!"

DON'T BE INVISIBLE

Most brands make what I call an invisible first impression. It's not that they make a bad first impression—but it's also not a good first impression. It's just invisible.

A nutritional supplement company we worked with introduced me to their line of products by saying they give their customers *more life and more fulfillment.* That sounds great but the same could be said of a church, an executive coach, a gym, or a daycare! Those words go in one ear and out the other and come off as standard marketing speak. It's an invisible first impression.

Consider all of the invisible first impressions you see as a consumer every day. How many billboards do you drive past that you pay no attention to? How many commercials run in the background of your TV or radio that you're tuning out? Think about how much money was spent to put those forgettable ads into the world.

Anecdotally, I'd say more than 50 percent of all advertising makes this mistake. They create invisible ads that nobody reads or cares about.

MARKETING MADE SIMPLE WILL CAUSE PEOPLE TO MEMORIZE YOUR OFFER

The one final thing a sales funnel needs to do is help your customers to memorize your offer.

Good marketing is an exercise in memorization and successful brands know it.

Repeating the same language in the same way in your one-liner, landing page, emails, and direct sales letters helps you brand yourself into your customer's mind.

We know that in only fifteen minutes, Geico can help us save up to 15 percent on car insurance. Why do we know this? Because their marketing led us through an exercise in memorization that caused us to memorize their offer.

After a customer has gone through your sales funnel, they will have memorized the talking points you want them to memorize. And when they've memorized your talking points, you will take up valuable real estate in their brains. They will know why you matter in their story, and they will be able to tell their friends why you matter in theirs too.

The key to going viral is to give people something very simple to think about and say regarding your products or services.

Before you create your sales funnel, come up with three or four things you want your customers to know about your brand.

If you understand the StoryBrand framework this is simple. Just use the words from your BrandScript to populate your sales funnel.

If you don't understand the StoryBrand framework, consider answering these questions in your sales funnel:

What problem do you solve for customers?

What will your customer's life look like if they buy your product?

What consequences does your product help customers avoid?

What does somebody need to do to buy your product? ("Click *buy* now?" "Call today?")

The answers to these questions should be short, simple, and easy to understand. Remember, customers do not move into confusion.

If you are a dentist, you might say:

Could your smile be better?

You could be happy with your smile.

✳ Schedule an appointment today.

I know that sounds simple, but we interact with thousands of brands who fail to tell their customers exactly what they offer and exactly how they can change their customers' lives for the better. In your marketing copy, don't be cute, be clear. Simplify your message and repeat it over and over using the same language and customers will finally figure out where you fit in their lives.

THE MARKETING
MADE SIMPLE CHECKLIST

Each sales funnel you create should break through the advertising clutter and speak directly to customers.

Your sales funnels are the foundation of your entire marketing effort. Again, once your sales funnels are created, your advertising campaigns should support those sales funnels, which then sell your product or service.

If you're a visual learner or are looking for inspiration, start there.

There are many kinds of sales funnels. If done well, they all work. The Marketing Made Simple Checklist is a collection of best practices we've learned, having helped more than ten thousand businesses create marketing campaigns that work.

The practical tools we will help you build will guide customers through the three stages of relationships. We'll help you create one-liners that pique a customer's curiosity, wireframe websites and landing pages that further intrigue them about the problems you solve, lead generators that enlighten them as to why your products and services will work for them, email campaigns that establish trust with customers, and sales emails and calls to action that ask for a commitment without making you sound like a sleazy salesperson.

The five pieces of your sales funnel will be:

Curiosity	Enlightenment	Commitment
One-Liner	Lead generators	Sales email campaigns
Website	Nuture email campaigns	

The next few chapters walk you step by step through how to create a marketing sales funnel. It is a checklist for you to walk through and make sure you have what you need and that you are doing it right.

You will start with building curiosity for your business through a one-liner and website wireframe. Then you will take your customer through the enlightenment phase by creating lead generators and nurture emails. Finally, you ask them to make a commitment with a sales email sequence. Each piece of collateral you create from the checklist will further engage your customer in a relationship with you and lead toward a sale.

So you know you are doing it right, each chapter contains an explanation of why you are creating the piece you are creating, a step-by-step guide to writing the material—and then we tell you how to implement it.

In the chapter on execution, we even give you a complete plan including a meeting schedule and agendas so that your team can create a series of sales funnels together.

EXECUTION IS KEY

We recently hired an independent research company to survey thousands of our customers to find out who sees greater success from clarifying their message and creating marketing that sells.

After all the surveys and all the data were compiled, you know what made the greatest difference? It wasn't size, background, education, or business type. The companies that showed the greatest growth in profit, saw greater ease in the creation of marketing collateral, and saved more time and money in creating marketing collateral were the ones who actually followed the exact plan I am going to walk you through. The only thing that had a statistical impact on growth was how they implemented the framework.

Bottom line: when customers were asked what level of success they saw compared to how much they implemented the checklist, there was a striking correlation between the level of success as compared with implementation across all channels of marketing. This pattern was the same across every individual area of marketing as well as overall implementation. It also influenced every area of success. While simply implementing one part of the checklist still showed positive results, higher levels of implementation resulted in more positive results. The more thoroughly an organization implemented the Marketing Made Simple Checklist, the more confidence employees had in creating marketing messaging, and the more time and money was saved in creating marketing collateral.

Most importantly, the more a company executed the Marketing Made Simple Checklist, the more money they made.

In the graphs below you can see clearly, the more you implement the checklist throughout your marketing, the more growth your company will see, the more confident your team will become in creating marketing, and the more time you will save.

The data shows that the Marketing Made Simple Checklist works and it works for everybody.

You just have to execute.

If you want J. J. and I to take you through the Marketing Made Simple Checklist in video format, visit BusinessMadeSimple.com and register for our very inexpensive online platform. Use the code "Marketing" to get a buy-one-gift-one offer, allowing you and your entire team to use the platform for half the cost.

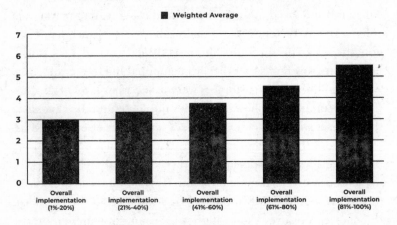

StoryBrand Messaging has directly contributed to our organization's growth.

Graph of relationship between implementation and growth

Whether you're going it alone with this book, hiring a guide, or learning from us on video, make a commitment today to follow through on this simple sales funnel and you will see results.

StoryBrand has made our team more confident.

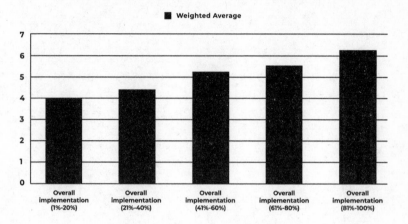

Graph of relationship between implementation and team confidence

StoryBrand has saved us time.

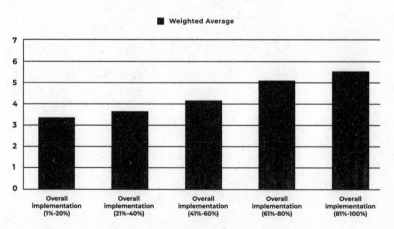

Graph of relationship between implementation and time saving

Part II

CREATE YOUR
MARKETING MADE
SIMPLE SALES FUNNEL

The second part of Marketing Made Simple is a step-by-step process that will walk you through the creation of five marketing tools you can use to build a sales funnel.

Again, the marketing tools you will create will be:

1. A one-liner
2. A website or landing page.
3. A lead-generating PDF
4. An email nurture campaign
5. An email sales campaign

Once you create these five pieces of marketing collateral and put them in play, your business will begin to grow.

Still, make a commitment now to finish the process. Whether you're the CEO or simply lead a department, learning to create sales funnels and executing this marketing plan puts you ahead of an overwhelming number of professional marketers. Most marketing agents believe marketing is an art, not a science. We disagree. While there is art involved, it is very much a science. A science you can learn.

From today on, I deputize you as a part-time marketer. Whatever your job description is, add "part-time marketer" to the end of it and get to work creating, perfecting, and executing this plan.

And don't forget to have fun.

Now, let's start creating a marketing plan that works.

4

CREATE
YOUR ONE-LINER

*The One Magical Sentence
That Will Grow Your Business*

Magic spells really do exist.

Remember when we were kids, playing around with the magic wand we made out of a stick in the backyard? We'd point it at the cat and tell the cat to become a rabbit, summoning the power of the cosmos with the magic words "hocus pocus."

I don't know about you, but my cat never turned into a rabbit.

I did manage to bring my sister's dead goldfish back to life one afternoon when we discovered it floating at the top of its bowl after church. It was quite a surprise. As I said a little prayer for it while digging a hole in the backyard with a spoon, it just started flopping.

Other than the goldfish incident (which to this day I consider more of a faith healing), I've had no success in magic.

I let the dream go when, wide eyed and with great focus, I was unable to get my great uncle to lift the lid of his casket at his own funeral.

So I stopped believing in magic.

Until.

Until I discovered the power of a one-liner.

WORDS MAKE WORLDS

Our entire world is made with words. Every manmade thing started with one person talking to another saying something like "what if we put a wall here?" or "let's paint it red."

Words create worlds—not only physical worlds but the worlds we perceive.

You and I perceive some people as more important than others, simply because somebody made up the words *king* and *queen* and attributed those words to people with a certain surname.

From words, the world as we know it fell into place. Hierarchies, housing markets, romances, and global agreements are all constructs made of words.

Appropriately, even Moses attributed the creation of our world to the breathy words of God.

The most infamous origin story of all time has God speaking us into existence.

There is no hammer, no knife, no excavator more powerful than a spoken word.

And yet every day we use them flippantly. The very words we could be using to build a better life we make no effort to channel.

WORDS PICK LOCKS

My friend Lanny developed the hobby of picking locks. He likes puzzles, both physical and mental, and said he took up picking locks as a way of resting his mind.

He actually bought a set of tools and a set of clear, glass locks so he could practice by seeing how his little tools worked to release the levers.

The hobby paid off. Several times each year he helps somebody get into their locked car or picks the lock on his hotel room door because he lost his key. Once, on a runway in Haiti, he picked the lock on an airplane because, no kidding, the pilot had locked himself out of his own plane!

The truth is I still don't believe in magic, but I do believe saying the right words in the right order can pick the lock in somebody's brain. We just need a little help. We need tools and a process.

The most powerful tool any of us can use to magically open doors is a one-liner.

THE WORDS THAT OPEN DOORS

A one-liner is a concise statement you can use to clearly explain what you offer. It is the most powerful tool you can use to make customers curious about your brand.

A one-liner makes people *lean in* rather than tune out at cocktail party.

The idea of a one-liner is unique to the Marketing Made Simple framework, but it didn't originate with us.

It comes from Hollywood.

When a screenwriter writes a film, she must also write a one-sentence description of the screenplay that makes investors want to take a risk on the story. After that story is turned into a full-length feature, that same one-liner is used to get you to go see the film.

Whenever you're scrolling through your phone deciding what movie you'd like to see tonight, you're reading through one-liners. Often called a logline, a one-liner is a one-statement description of the story you are inviting people to experience.

If the one-liner is confusing or elusive, it will cost the producers millions at the box office.

A bad one-liner can sink a film, no matter how good that film may be.

Just like some businesspeople are better at creating products than marketing them, some screenwriters are better at creating a film than they are at describing what the story is or why it matters.

But to be a financial success, we all need to be good at both.

HERE'S HOW TO CREATE YOUR ONE-LINER

The one-liner is composed of three parts—the problem, the solution, and the result.

Let's take a look at what you need to do to create a home run one-liner.

The structure:

Step 1: Problem

When you're describing the story you're inviting customers into, always start with the problem.

The problem is the hook. If a story doesn't have a problem, the story never gets started.

Here's an example:

Yesterday morning I woke up, went into the kitchen, and turned on the coffee maker. I waited for the coffee maker to finish brewing the coffee and then poured enough into a cup to get the day going. I sat down at the table in the kitchen, drank my coffee, and read through the morning paper...

Now technically, that's a story. It has a character who is doing something. The problem is, it's not a very interesting story. In fact, as you read it, you were likely wondering when the story was going to get started.

But that's not what you were really waiting for. What you were really waiting for was for something to challenge the protagonist.

When we're waiting for a story get started, we're really waiting for a problem the hero has to overcome. We're waiting for something tough or difficult or scary or painful to happen.

A good storyteller knows to get to the problem fast, otherwise they will lose the audience.

The same is true when we're talking about our businesses. We need to get to the problem fast.

Let's try that story again.

Yesterday morning I woke up and went into the kitchen to turn on the coffee maker. As I turned the corner to the kitchen I saw several broken glasses on the floor and cereal spread all over the kitchen. Then, out of nowhere, a squirrel drops down from the chandelier above the kitchen island!

Now that's a decent start to a story. We're interested. The story only gets started when you state the problem.

Stating the Problem Adds Value to Your Products

Imagine being at a cocktail party and meeting two different people who had similar private chef businesses.

When you ask the first person what they do, they tell you they are a private chef. You curiously inquire how they got started, who they have cooked for, and the conversation quickly turns to the chef's favorite restaurants in the area. It never occurs to you that you might need their services.

But then you meet another private chef, and when you ask what she does she says:

"You know how most families hardly eat together anymore and when they do, they don't eat as healthy as they should? I'm a private chef…"

The second chef is way more interesting. In fact, as she talks, you start picturing her in your home, cooking meals for your family.

Why?

Because she stated the problem she solves before she stated the solution (her service.)

The other reason a one-liner starts with a problem is because stating the problem adds perceived value to the product.

Stating the Problem Is a Way to
Be Remembered in Your Customer's Mind

Always start your one-liner by stating the problem.

What's the obvious response when your coworker tells you he has a headache?

- ▶ Coworker: "I have a headache."
- ▶ You: "Do you want an Advil?"

You rarely think of a brand unless you associate that brand with the solution to a problem.

If you want to be remembered, associate your product or service with the solution to a problem.

Why start your one-liner by stating a problem? (1) Because the problem is the hook, (2) because the problem adds value to your product or service, and (3) because stating the problem is a great way to be remembered in your customer's mind.

Exercise

Start off by stating the problem or pain point that most of your clients face.

Example from the StoryBrand one-liner: Most business leaders struggle to talk about what they do.

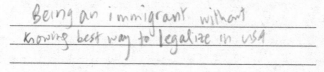

Being an immigrant without knowing best way to legalize in USA

Other Examples:

Dentist's office: Most parents get stressed when they think about taking their child to the dentist.

Nashville bike store: With 110 people moving to Nashville every day, people are wasting more and more time every day sitting in traffic.

Marketing agency: Most businesses lack the time and expertise to build a website that gets results.

Things to Consider

1. The biggest mistake companies make in creating this section is not actually starting with a problem. I know that sounds obvious, but it happens all the time. Make sure the first statement is a clear problem and make sure it is a pain people actually feel.
2. Do not try to include every problem your customer faces in your one-liner. Name only one problem and

make it the one the most people feel. This is not the space to talk about every problem you solve. This is the hook to get people curious. You can talk about other problems in other parts of the sales funnel, but in a one-liner you want to talk about only one.

3. Make sure the problem you start with is a problem that your company can actually solve. Your customer may be facing many problems, but if you can't solve those problems, don't talk about them.

4. Think about how you are different than your competition. If you are a part of a crowded industry, talk about a problem your competition creates with their services. Use this space as a place to differentiate from the competition.

Step 2: Solution

Now that you've opened a story loop by stating a problem, your customer is ready to hear about a solution.

Stating the problem first will increase the perceived value of the solution you offer.

We are all in business because we provide the solution to a problem. Every single product you buy you buy only because it solves a problem.

The second statement in your one-liner, then, should sound like a reveal. As the customer listens (or reads) about the problem, they begin to wonder how this problem can be resolved. A subtle anticipation then grows in your customer's mind and they lean in (rather than tune out) when you let them know what you offer.

Make Sure the Problem and Solution Are Connected

When creating their one-liners, many people fail to connect the problem and solution. They will say something like this:

Many people struggle with fatigue in the middle of the day. Our patented vitamin formula was created by ten of the world's most recognized nutritionists...

The fact a group of nutritionists created your vitamin formula does not clearly explain how it solves your customer's problem.

I know it's tempting to talk about how your grandfather started the company or that you've won all kinds of awards, but don't fall for it. In your one-liner, you simply want to state how you resolve the customer's problem.

Let's try that again:

Many people struggle with fatigue in the middle of the day. We've created a vitamin formula that gives you balanced energy from morning till night....

The part about the nutritionist can come later in the conversation. But don't miss your chance to clearly state the problem and solution so that the first impression of your product or service sticks.

Close the Story Loop

Another mistake some people make in stating the solution to the problem they solve is they become too wordy.

You don't need to write a play.

The danger with using too many words is that your statement may open up too many story loops.

The job of the second component of your one-liner is to close the story loop, not open more.

Statements like "Our GPS technology allows our driverless lawnmower to be guided by ten different satellites" are going to invite a ton of questions about satellites and robots, unlike a statement such as "Our lawnmower works like a Roomba in that it safely cuts your lawn without you having to break a sweat."

Don't Get Cute or Clever

Cute and clever language is almost always the enemy of clarity. Clarity sells, while cute and clever confuse.

Often, the solution can simply be the product itself.

These are great examples:

We have a new medicine for migraine headaches.

Our trucks run on natural gas.

The shingles we install on your roof last a lifetime and are guaranteed to never leak.

These simple statements work terrifically to sell products. But you'd be shocked at how few businesses actually state their solutions so simply.

Instead, we hear statements like "Make migraines a memory" or "Fuel efficiency for the future" or "Rain ought to stay on the outside of your house!"

None of those cute and clever statements will sell anything.

Don't let yourself overthink the solution component of your one-liner. The solution is the easiest part. It's your product.

State the product clearly, and after hearing the problem you solve, your customers will begin to associate you and your product with a solution to their problem.

When stating the solution to your customer's problem do three things:

- ▸ Connect the solution directly to the problem.
- ▸ Close the story loop.
- ▸ Avoid using cute and clever language as a substitute for clarity.

Exercise

Talk about your solution to the problem you just stated.

Example from the StoryBrand one-liner: At Story-Brand we've created a communication framework that helps people clarify their message.

_____

_____

_____

_____

Other Examples:

Dentist's office: At Kid's Teeth, our fun and welcoming office puts kids at ease.

Nashville bike store: Nashville Bike Store will fit you with a Circuit E-bike.

Marketing agency: At John Doe Marketing we'll build you an amazing website at an affordable price.

Things to Consider

1. Keep it simple. Companies often make the mistake of using inside language that is hard to understand and sounds awkward when saying it out loud. Make sure this section is something that is easy to repeat and very clear.
2. Use your name in the solution. By including your company name in the solution, you are associating your brand with the problem you solve.

3. Make sure your solution is connected to the problem you just stated. The one-liner has to be cohesive.
4. Do not try to explain everything you do for your customer in this section. This is a short, clear description of what service you offer.

Step 3: Result

The final part of the one-liner is the part everybody's been waiting for.

Every word, every image, and every beat in a movie is heading toward a specific scene. Sometimes called the climactic scene or the obligatory scene, this all-important scene happens at the end of the movie and it's the scene that resolves all the conflict: Tommy Boy saves his father's company. Rudy finally gets to play football for Notre Dame. Erin Brockovich wins the court case.

The third part of your one-liner should release all the tension you created in the first section.

The Problem, Solution, and Result Should Connect

When writing their one-liners, many people fail to connect the problem, solution, and result.

For instance:

Many families struggle to spend time together, but at Acorn Family Camp, we solve the problem of boring summers so families create memories that last.

That sounds good, but look a little closer. The problem was that families don't spend time together, but the solution was about summers being boring. It works okay, but when you connect all three, it works even better.

Example:

Many families struggle to spend time together, but at Acorn Family Camp time stands still and families create connections that last a lifetime.

Can you see the difference? When the three components connect, the story resolves and the hearer gets that little jolt of pleasure that comes with clarity.

Keep Asking "Which Results In..." to Get to Your Solution

When you write the solution part of your one-liner, you'll want to get all the way to the end result your customer will experience. And you want that result to be tangible. Make it something they can see or feel.

If you're a roofer, you might be tempted to say "you'll get a good roof," but if you add the "which results in" question at the end of your statement, maybe you can take it even further.

Example: You'll get a good roof which results in a worry-free home.

There you go. Now you know what you're really selling. You're really selling a worry-free home.

Exercise →

Clearly explain how your customer will feel and what they get after you solve their problem.

Example from the StoryBrand one-liner: When you clarify your message word starts to spread about your company and your business grows.

_____

_____

_____

_____

Other Examples:

Dentist's office: so they aren't afraid and their parents actually enjoy their dentist visit.

Nashville bike store: and you'll get hours back in your day and get to work faster.

Marketing agency: so you can stand out from the competition and get more leads that turn into customers.

Things to Consider

1. Make sure the success you talk about is directly related to the problem stated earlier. This keeps the story cohesive and shows the customer how their life will be better after you solve their problem.
2. The success should be about your customer, not your company. The one-liner should not end with something like "we can help you" or "and then you will be our favorite customer." Speak to what their life is like after doing business with you, not what you do or how good you are.
3. Commas are not your friend. You may have a ton of success that you would like to add here. Keep it simple and compelling. By putting too much success in you actually end up diluting your brand. Focus on one or two success points and leave it at that.

4. Do not overpromise. Any success you state here should be something you are able to deliver.

Now, Let's Put It All Together:

Example from the StoryBrand one-liner: Most business leaders struggle to talk about what they do, so we've created a communication framework that helps people clarify their message. When you clarify your message, word starts to spread about your company and your business grows.

_____

_____

_____

_____

Other Examples

Dentist's office: Most parents get stressed when they think about taking their child to the dentist. At Kid's Teeth, our fun and welcoming office puts kids at ease so they aren't afraid and their parents actually enjoy their dentist visit.

Nashville bike store: With 110 people moving to Nashville every day, people are wasting more and more time every day sitting in traffic. With a Circuit E-bike fitted just for you, you'll get hours back in your day and get to work faster.

Marketing agency: Most businesses lack the time and expertise to build a website that gets results. At John Doe Marketing we'll build you an amazing website at an affordable price so you can stand out from the competition and get more leads that turn into customers.

Things to Consider

1. After putting all the parts together, make sure it not only makes sense but sounds good when said out loud. Sometimes what looks good on paper does not translate well when spoken. Say it out loud and see how it sounds.
2. Don't be afraid to change things up after it is all together. You want to make sure you have all three parts in this specific order, but don't be afraid to get a little creative.
3. Make sure it is easily repeatable. If after you put it all together it is hard to memorize or cumbersome, go back and simplify it so that everyone on your team can say it easily.
4. Check to make sure it is simple. If you tell someone your one-liner and they have to ask "what do you mean?" about any of the sections, then you are too complicated. Go back and make sure each section is clear. Refining is your friend.

WHAT TO DO WITH THE ONE-LINER

One-liners are one of the most powerful tools we give to our clients. We've watched clients improve sales dramatically, simply by creating a one-liner and putting it to work.

Once your one-liner is refined, memorize it. Have your entire team memorize it.

When everyone on your team can repeat the one-liner, your entire staff is transformed into a salesforce.

Other Ways to Use Your One-Liner

Below are a few ways you can put your one-liner to use right away.

- ▶ Put it on the back of your business card.
- ▶ Make it your email signature.
- ▶ Print it on your wall in your retail space.
- ▶ Make it the first sentence in the paragraph on your *about us* section on your website.
- ▶ Use it for your profile descriptions on social media.

You'd be surprised how many opportunities you're missing to spread the word about what you do. Whether you're on an airplane, at a cocktail party, or even a family gathering, when we explain what we do using a tiny short story, people pay attention.

You'll be able to use your one-liner on your website, in emails, keynotes, and elevator pitches. Your one-liner will be the central component to your entire messaging campaign.

Now that you've created your one-liner, you know what you offer your customers and can say it in clear, repeatable language. That's half the battle.

When you start implementing your one-liner, you'll start seeing an increase in sales. Everywhere you put (or say) your one-liner is like a hook in the water. You should start catching more fish.

Make sure to visit MarketingMadeSimple.com to download a free "blank" sales funnel you can physically create on paper. Work with your designer to execute your sales funnel or visit MarketingMadeSimple.com to hire a certified StoryBrand guide who can create a sales funnel for you.

5

A WIREFRAMED
WEBSITE THAT WORKS

Once a customer gets curious about how you can solve their problem, they may come looking for more information.

This is where your website comes in.

A great website can be worth hundreds of thousands or even millions of dollars. The problem is too many brands are getting their websites wrong, and they don't know why.

IT'S ALL IN THE WORDS

Most of us intuitively know our website is important so we pay somebody thousands to design it for us.

Inevitably, whoever designs our website is more concerned with colors, images, and "feel" than they are with the words we are using. And while colors and images and feel are fine, it's words that sell things.

Your website needs to include words that sell.

At the StoryBrand marketing workshop, we take an hour or so at the end of the second day to put a handful of client websites on the big screen, and I offer custom feedback.

I've done this for thousands of brands and most of them are making the same mistakes.

Here are a list of avoidable mistakes you're likely making on your website:

- ▶ You are using too much insider language
- ▶ You are using too many words in the header.
- ▶ The call to action buttons use passive language.
- ▶ The call to action buttons are not repeated down the page
- ▶ The images do not relate to the product or back up the words you're using on the page.
- ▶ The language is cute or clever but not clear.
- ▶ The site does not promote a lead generator.
- ▶ You're using a slide show so the text changes too fast and frustrates potential customers.
- ▶ The site tells *your* story rather than inviting customers into a story.

The biggest mistake clients make when it comes to websites is making them too complicated.

Most businesses need a website that serves a single purpose: it creates sales.

Creating sales may not be the main reason you are in business, but it *is* the main reason you will stay in business.

Your website should be a sales machine.

WIREFRAME A WEBSITE THAT WORKS

Sadly, when most people hire somebody to create their website, the designer asks them all sorts of personal questions. They ask what their favorite colors are, their favorite music, how and why they started the company, and so on.

These are the wrong questions to ask. This designer, sadly, thinks he or she is preparing you for a banquet in which you are receiving an award.

Your website is not a place for you to celebrate yourself. Your website is a place where you sell your customer a product that solves their problem and makes their lives better.

The right questions a designer should be asking are:

What is the problem you solve?

How does your customer feel after you solve their problem?

How does somebody usually buy your product?

Was there unforeseen value that was added to your customer's life when you bought this product?

START WITH A WIREFRAME

If a marketer asks the right questions, they can create a site that uses words that move more of your products.

But let's not have them lay out that expensive website just yet. Let's start with a wireframe.

A wireframe is a long piece of paper (or digital page) that includes the text in a rough-draft drawing of what the website might look like.

After your designer does an intake, they should turn in a wireframe. The wireframe is going to allow you to review the site and perhaps even get feedback before you spend hard-earned money creating a permanent site.

Remember, words on a website sell products. It's great if the site is beautiful, but without the right words, the site won't sell anything.

Settle on the right words by creating a wireframe that works. Get it all down on paper before you design that site and you'll thank me. The last thing you want to do is create and re-create a website a thousand times through a process of trial and error.

If there is a proven way to create websites that work, why don't we just create one for ourselves?

HOW TO WIREFRAME A WEBSITE

Before you spend thousands to redesign your website, read all the way though this chapter and complete the exercises.

By the time you're finished you will have a completed wireframe you can take to your designer.

No more wasting money on beautiful websites that don't impact sales.

Nine Sections of a Website That Work

It is absolutely possible that a website can be a great work of art and also dramatically increase your sales. That said, too many businesses spend thousands on a website that, ultimately, is simply a great work of art and doesn't affect their sales at all.

These people are proprietors of the arts. They might as well print out a copy of their website, frame it, have their so-called marketer sign it, and then hang it above their fireplace.

If you can create an artistic, beautiful website that still sells, that's terrific. But in my view, the artistic statement is icing on the cake. I want your website to grow your business.

There are nine sections of a website that we've seen increase sales time and time again. Each of these sections are like hooks in the pond: the more of them you include, the more fish you will catch.

The sections of a website I will help you create are:

- ▶ **The Header.** The very top of your website, in which you use *very few* words to let people know what you offer.
- ▶ **The Stakes.** The section of the website in which you explain what you are saving customers from.
- ▶ **The Value Proposition.** The section of a website in which you add value to your product or service by listing its benefits.
- ▶ **The Guide.** The section of the website in which you introduce yourself as the brand or person who can solve your customer's problem.
- ▶ **The Plan.** The part where you reveal the path a customer must take to do business with you and solve their problem.
- ▶ **The Explanatory Paragraph.** A long-form BrandScript in which you invite your customers into a story. This is also where you will improve your SEO.
- ▶ **The Video (optional).** A video in which you reiterate much of what was on the website in more dynamic form.
- ▶ **Price Choices (optional):** The divisions of your company or your list of products.
- ▶ **Junk Drawer.** The most important part of your website, because it's where you're going to list everything you previously thought was important.

What Order Do They Go In?

I often get asked, "What order would be put these sections in?"

With the exception of the header going at the top, there is no magical order. There are an infinite number of possibilities, and honestly, it's pretty hard to screw up.

Think of designing of website like writing a song. Each section of the website is a different chord on the guitar. I am teaching you how to play the chords. How you use the chords, what order they go in, and how long you play them is up to you. Your job is to take these chords and make your website into a beautiful song.

At our marketing workshops, we go through a similar process. At the end of a couple short hours, the hundreds of businesses leaders in the room have wireframed a website that will work. After they wireframe these different sections, they can move them around intuitively to get the flow right.

Take a few hours and complete each section of your website. Try not to skip a section because you'll be surprised at what you come up with when you give it a little time.

Also, make this a multiday process. Often I wireframe a website in phases. My first draft is just that, it's a first draft. Then, after a night's sleep, I see more clearly how I should structure my site.

With that, let's get started with the fun part. Let's wireframe the different sections of your website.

Section 1: The Header

You only get one chance to make a first impression. The header is the top section of your website and the first impression a customer has about your product or service.

You do not get two chances to make a first impression, so getting it right is important.

According to Chao Liu and colleagues from Microsoft Research, the first ten seconds a potential customer lands on the page are the most critical for users' decision to stay or leave.

If your website survives the first ten seconds, users will look around a little bit longer. This, of course, translates into either building a relationship with a customer and growing your business or losing that relationship and allowing your business to decline.

Because you only have ten seconds (Liu also found the amount of time you have decreases every year), we are going to have to use words that pique our customers' curiosity.

Again, what will pique their curiosity? They will get curious about you only if they think the products or services you provide might help them survive.

Does Your Header Pass the Grunt Test?

When we train our StoryBrand certified guides, we repeat over and over that cute and clever don't sell products, clarity sells products.

Amateur copywriters and marketers try to make a first impression by branding themselves as cute, clever, or interesting. While there is nothing wrong with being cute, clever, or interesting, if cute, clever, and interesting come at the cost of clarity, you'll lose.

To make sure your website makes a terrific first impression and piques your customers' curiosity, make sure your header passes the grunt test.

What is the grunt test?

Passing the grunt test ensures your website speaks to the lowest common denominator about what you do well.

Remember, marketing is an exercise in memorization. That means you have to speak in simple, clear language. And that language needs to tell people how you can help them survive.

Imagine a caveman sitting in a cave by a fire. He's a simple fellow, but not stupid. He's busy defending his tribe, hunting for food for his family, and sewing the latest bearskin fashions so he fits in with his peers.

Let's say in our imaginary universe the caveman could look at your website. But only for ten seconds.

Could that caveman grunt the answer to these three questions:

1. What do you offer?
2. How will it make his customer life better?
3. What does he need to do to buy it?

If a caveman can grunt the answers to these three questions, you're on to something.

You don't have access to a caveman, of course. But you do have access to lots of other smart, busy people who, because they are constantly filtering out information, will need to answer those three questions just as quickly.

When wireframing a website, in fact, we recommend going to a coffee shop and asking a couple people to take a look at your header. I know it's uncomfortable to talk to a stranger, but whether or not a couple of strangers can say what you offer, how it will make their lives better, and what they can do to buy it could make or cost you millions.

Remember, clarity is the key.

Let's look at each of the three questions that will allow you to pass the grunt test a little more closely:

Question 1: What Do You Offer?

What is the physical, tangible thing you are selling?

You'd be shocked at how many corporations don't say what they sell right at the top of their website. Or, worse, they think they're saying it but really they're being elusive.

A financial advisory may offer "A path to a better future" without realizing that could be confused for a gym, a college, a church, or just about anything else.

Don't use the header of your website to differentiate yourself from somebody else. Clarity itself is going to differentiate you—because your competition, I guarantee you, is being confusing.

Often, a client will try to explain what they offer in complicated, poetic language. But what their customer is really looking for is a short explanation of what they offer in layman's terms.

What is your product or service?

- ▶ Lawn care
- ▶ Coaching
- ▶ Copywriting
- ▶ Clothing
- ▶ Haircuts and color

Take a minute and write down a clear and concise statement of what you offer.

_____

_____

_____

_____

Question 2: How Will It Make Your Customer's Life Better?

Once you have clearly explained what you offer, let's sweeten the deal.

If somebody buys what you offer, how will it make their lives better?

You don't have space here to list a thousand ways that your product or service makes life better—even though that might be true. For clarity and brevity's sake, you'll have to choose the one most significant way your client's lives will improve, and trust that choosing one will be remembered while listing many would be forgotten.

How does your customer's life improve because they do business with you? Do they have more money? More time? A higher status in life? More peace? Better relationships?

You will have space later to expand on other areas you improve their lives, but for the purpose of the header, lets choose one.

_____

_____

_____

_____

Compile your answers to the past two questions into a single statement like one of these:

1. Injury lawyers committed to helping you get your life back
2. Great managers aren't born, they're trained: See how we do it
3. Transform your health, regain your life: a proven, drug-free path of healing for all of your unresolved health concerns
4. Surprise and delight your guests with handcrafted desserts

Your statement below:

_____

_____

_____

_____

Question 3: What Do They Need to Do to Buy It?

You'd be surprised how many people don't have a "buy now" button anywhere on their website.

You can tell they've spent days, months, weeks, years even working to make their website functional and beautiful and make sure it represents them well.

Then they send their customers away without even asking them to buy anything.

The "buy now," "schedule a call," or "shop now" buttons are the cash registers of your online store.

Some business leaders don't want to appear pushy. I understand the feeling. The last thing I want to do is strong-arm my customers into buying from me. That said, not having a clear call to action is the equivalent of telling customers you don't really believe in your product and don't think that product can solve their problems and change their lives.

Imagine walking through a clothing store and picking out several items you'd like to buy. When you walk to the front of the store to buy the items, though, you don't find a person behind a cash register. You walk around the store wondering where you can buy the items before finally stopping to talk to a team member.

"Oh, we hate bothering people with all that corporate nonsense. We're about so much more than selling clothes, you know."

"Right, but I want to buy these things. How do I buy them?"

"Oh, that's easy. There's a lady who will take your money in the second stall of the lady's bathroom. Like I said, we don't want to appear too corporate."

This interaction would be absurd, of course. And yet many online businesses treat their customers exactly this way. In the end, not being clear and direct in your calls to action comes off as either passive or self-obsessed.

What the customer really needs is a clear cash register so they know where to go when they decide to make a purchase.

If a user lands on your site and wants to purchase your product or service, what is the next step you want them to take?

Can they buy your product now? Do they need to be added to a wait list? Do they need to set up an appointment? Should they call? Register? Sign up? Donate?

Don't Be Passive-Aggressive

Calls to action like "Learn more," "Find out about us," "Curious?" or "Our Process" are weak and confusing.

What a customer really needs is something to accept or reject. Until then, they are confused about what you want them to do or where you want this relationship to go.

Often we use passive language like "learn more" or "get started" because we don't want to push people. We may use this approach because relationships with our customers are important to us and we want to make sure to position ourselves as friends.

Being friends with your customers is a great idea, but don't forget, this is a business relationship and business relationships are, by nature, transactional. And there is nothing wrong with a transactional business relationship.

You certainly want to be kind and respectful to your customers and even friendly, but in the end, trying to be their friend while passively trying to get them to buy from you is just creepy.

Make your intentions known early and often. Use a strong call to action.

Below, list how I can purchase your product. What is your call to action button going to say?

_____

_____

_____

_____

Where Does Your Call to Action Button Go on the Website?

When visitors land on your desktop website, their eyes read your page in either a Z pattern or an F pattern. Different studies have revealed different patterns, but regardless, visitors' eyes do not move randomly across the page.

We teach our marketers to place important text and important calls to action along the path that the human eye travels when glancing at a website. Meaning, their eyes are drawn to the top left of the website first, then scan across to the top right, then diagonally down and across the middle of the page to the bottom left and then back across to the bottom right.

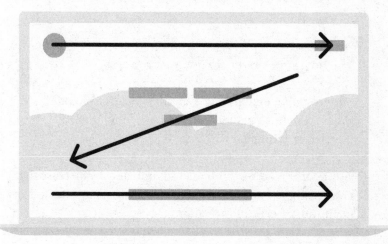

There are two places we recommend placing direct and transitional calls to action. The first is at the top right of the page, which is by far the most valuable real estate on your webpage. The second is directly in the middle of the header beneath your headline and subtitle.

■　■　■

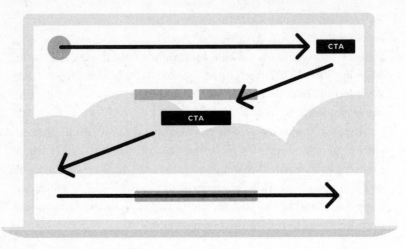

By repeating the call to action twice, even in the header, you will be letting your customer know that you are:

1. Interested in establishing a business relationship and
2. You'd like to solve their problem by selling them a service or product.

Many people reading this book will dramatically increase their sales by getting rid of passive language on their website and replacing it with direct calls to action.

Choose Your Images Carefully

While your wireframe won't have any images, you'll want to choose your images carefully.

Few images work better than smiling, happy people enjoying your products. So if you can't figure out what images to use, smiling happy people are a good place to start.

Avoid creating a slide show in your header in which different text and images continuously change. Customers rarely have time to read one message before it's changed to another, and after about three of these sliding messages, they tend to forget all of them.

Looping images (silent film) are terrific on websites but make sure the text that floats over those images is fixed. Branding is all about repeating the same simple message over and over until your customers have it memorized. Sliding text, then, hurts rather than contributes to your branding effort.

Let's Build Your Header

Let's put the three components of the grunt test together and build the header on your new website.

Write out the headline for your header, plus a subtitle if you need one, and write your direct call to action in the empty boxes below.

In the parentheses, describe what image (or looping film) you'd like to use in your header. If you build playgrounds, show children enjoying playing on your equipment. If you bake cakes, show some of those beautiful cakes being decorated and happy customers picking them up and gazing at them in wonder. Don't

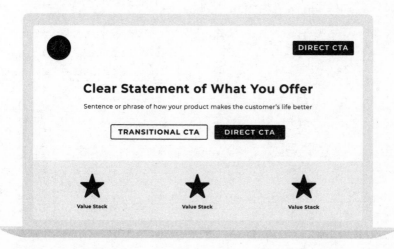

worry about taking pictures just yet. You'll do that later. Right now, decide what kind of images would best sell your product or service and describe those images in the header.

Next, list your calls to action. Your actual website may include both direct and transitional calls to action (we will cover transitional calls to action in the next chapter), but for now, consider this a simple drawing toward your header.

Now it's your turn. Fill in the box below.

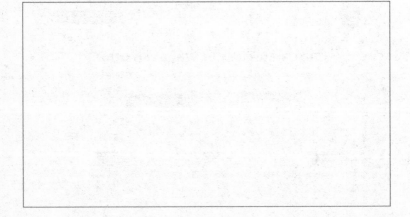

Check your work.

Imagine walking down to the local coffee shop with the header you just sketched. If you were to tap the first person you see on the shoulder, show it to them, and give them ten seconds to look at the page would they be able to say what you offer, how it will make their lives better, and what they'd need to do to buy it?

If so, your header passes the grunt test.

If you get the header of your website right, you're 50 percent done with your website. Yes, you have a lot of other sections to create, but that's how important your header is. It's up to 50 percent responsible for whether a customer spends any more time on your site and eventually makes a purchase.

Tomorrow morning, go back over your header. Fine tune the text and images. Survey a group of friends and perhaps even ask a stranger or two for feedback.

When you get the header right, your business has no choice but to grow!

From here on out, the order of the sections of your website matters a little less. If you structure your website in the exact order we lay out these sections, you'll do fine, but it's hardly necessary.

That said, I really love making the second section of the website illustrate the stakes. Showing what can be won or lost depending on whether I do business with you is a great way to add some drama into the story you are inviting customers to live.

Visit MarketingMadeSimple.com to download a free "blank" sales funnel you can physically create on paper. Work with your designer to execute your sales funnel or visit MarketingMadeSimple.com to hire a certified StoryBrand guide who can create a sales funnel for you.

■　　■　　■

Section 2: The Stakes

This is the Failure section. Stories love tension. A story without stakes is no story at all.

For example, let me tell you a story and you try to figure out how we can make the story a little better:

A young man wakes up in his Venice Beach apartment, opens the windows, and breathes in the fresh, ocean air. He makes a cup of coffee and sits down to read the morning paper. Just as he opens the paper, though, his best friend calls and lets him know that he and another group of friends are playing volleyball down on the beach.

The young man loves to play beach volleyball so he folds his paper and heads down to the beach. They play several games of volleyball, each ending in a tie when one of the guys says he's getting pretty hungry. The young man let them know there is a new taco shop across the street and suggest they try it out. They walk over to the taco shop and, amazingly, tacos are buy-one-get-one free and so, together, they devour several of them...

Okay, technically, that's a story. It's a story about a guy who wants to play volleyball and then wants to eat tacos.

The problem is, it's not a very interesting story. In fact, some of you read that story and wondered to yourself "when is this story going to get started?"

A story that fails to get started always has the same problem: there is no conflict!

A story gets started and hooks the reader the second the character experiences conflict.

In fact, most stories start with a character who wants something followed by a scene in which an enormous challenge is placed between where the character is and what the character wants. It's the crossing of that distance that makes the story work.

If our hero in the above story were to walk down to the beach for a game of volleyball only to experience a terrible earthquake in which the beach opened up and swallowed the other team, we'd have a story!

If a positive scene followed by a negative scene is how enthralling movies work, then why not follow the same formula on our website?

The first section of the website told our customers what their lives could look like if they purchased our product or service. Let's make the second section of our website speak to the current pain our customers are experiencing because they haven't bought our products yet.

What Is the Cost of Not Doing Business With You?

When you help your clients understand how much it is costing them to live without your products, the perceived value of those products increases.

Years ago when I first started StoryBrand, I asked an outside consultant to look over our website and offer constructive criticism. The consultant I'd chosen had attended our workshops and was familiar with our messaging framework. After looking at our site, though, she said we weren't following our own advice.

"What do you mean?" I asked.

"You talk about how important it is to include stakes, to demonstrate the cost of *not* doing business with you, but there isn't a single mention of the stakes on your site."

She then sent me a paragraph and told me to place it directly over the section of the website where we let people know how much the workshop costs.

The paragraph that she sent asked our customers a series of pointed questions about their messaging. It asked our customers if they were confusing their own customers and losing them in the process. This is how it read:

LIVE WORKSHOP

What's My Investment?

How much is **unclear messaging** costing you? How many potential customers **can't hear your offer** in the sea of noise? How many of your events are **half empty** because people don't know why they should come? How many people are **passing up your consulting**? Can potential customers understand why they need your product or service? A lack of clarity may already be **costing you** a great deal.

I asked our designer to include the new paragraph but I didn't feel good about it. I told my wife that night that it just didn't sound like our voice. We don't strong-arm customers into doing business with us. It's not who we are.

Betsy, my wife, said that if it bothered me so much I should ask our designer to remove the paragraph the next day.

I walked into our designer's office the next day and asked her opinion about the paragraph. She understood how I was feeling. It didn't quite feel like our voice.

"However," she said with a smile. "We did get five new orders last night!"

That paragraph is still on our site all these years later.

Why? Because story is a trustworthy guide. And if there are not stakes in a story, there is no story.

At our workshops, I teach that in a story there must always be pain and conflict, and yet when we talk about painful things in our marketing it can feel a little heavy. But don't be tricked into telling a boring story. The stakes matter, and if you don't let people know what pain you are helping them avoid you'll lull them to sleep rather than stimulate them to place orders.

What pain are you helping customers avoid? What pain are they currently dealing with that will be ended if they buy your products or service?

Some examples are:

- More wasted time
- Missed opportunities
- Lost business .
- Embarrassment
- Loss of sleep
- Frustration
- Weight gain
- Confusion
- Isolation
- Lack of access
- Lack of guidance
- Loss of status
- Not reaching potential
- Losing to the competition

When It Comes to Communicating the Stakes, Just a Little Bit Goes a Long Way

Unlike talking about our customers' potential success, the negative stakes in the story we are inviting customers into can be overdone.

We definitely want to include negative stakes on our website, but don't overdo it. When we get too negative, our customers will begin to tune us out. The brain is only willing to go so far before it decides it would rather live in a happy world, even if that world is a fictional construct.

I like to look at the components of a clear message like ingredients in a cake. To make a cake, you need cups and cups of flour (success) but only a tablespoon of salt (negative stakes). If you use too much salt, you ruin the cake, but if you leave it out, the whole thing tastes bland.

The singer Sarah McLachlan used to show up on television every once in a while as a spokesperson for the ASPCA. In her sweet, soft voice she'd talk about the plight of neglected and abandoned dogs while images of these adorable but sad animals slid across the screen.

When it comes to dogs, I'm about as sensitive as they come but even I couldn't face that commercial. I'd always change the channel as fast as possible. My wife and I donate to our local dog shelter and have rescued a dog ourselves, but having to face those sad eyes was too much!

My guess is that commercial did pretty well for the ASPCA, but I also believe if they'd have shown happy dogs in a home with only a pinch of sad dogs being abused, they'd have done even better. After all, the purpose of negative stakes in a story is to contrast with the happy ending we all want to experience.

What Are You Helping Customers Overcome or Avoid?

Without overdoing it or exaggerating the stakes, what kinds of problems are you helping customers overcome or avoid?

Examples:

1. No more sleepless nights, tossing and turning on a mattress that doesn't work for you.
2. Most people don't realize how much time they're wasting in their email inbox every day. We have a solution.
3. We meet people all the time who are wasting their money because they don't know how to invest it.
4. Are you tired of paying money for marketing that doesn't get results?

There are many ways to illustrate the stakes section of your website. You can include a few sentences describing the pain you help customers avoid, you can include a testimonial in which a customer explains how you helped them overcome a challenge, or you can simply list the problems you resolve in bullet points.

Here are some examples of stakes as they may appear on a website:

Parenting a late talker is tough.

When your child "should be talking by now," it's easy to get frustrated and overwhelmed—and to feel guilty for those emotions. You start to wonder if you've done something wrong as a parent.

Can we ease your mind a bit? The truth is, it really is frustrating and overwhelming trying to parent a late-talking child. Also, it's totally normal to worry about your child's development. You're not a bad parent. **And you're not alone.**

You just need the right tools so you can be the confident parent of a talkative child.

We have the tools you need. As certified speech-language pathologists, our team has worked with thousands of parents just like you—parents who just want to help their children talk, but nothing's working. Our online course teaches you simple speech secrets so you can help your child communicate.

> **BUY NOW ($99)**   **LEARN MORE**

Have you been frustrated by brokers who:

- ✔ Don't communicate with you?
- ✔ Make big promises but don't deliver?
- ✔ Cost you time and money with deals that fall through?
- ✔ Don't know the local area or local buyers?
- ✔ Think "list it on MLS" = effective marketing?
- ✔ Aren't in any hurry to sell your property?

> At MANSARD we'll market your property like it's our own.

What pain or problems are you helping your customers avoid? List the pain points and challenges you resolve in the section below:

_____

_____

_____

_____

Again, you can be creative in how you illustrate the stakes on your website. Is it a checklist, a sentence, a series of questions, bullet points? Take a moment and sketch out what this section could look like.

Section 3: The Value Proposition

What could your customers life look like if they bought your product or service? Like I said earlier, from here on out you can put the sections of your website in any order you like. But one reason I like putting the value proposition third is because it follows the positive and negative flow we often see in stories.

Stories love to demonstrate contrasts. One character will be blunt and off-putting, and the character standing next to her will be kind and gentle. One scene will be visually dark and brooding, and the next will be bright and airy.

You'll notice contrast the most, though, in the positive and negative movements of the screenplay. Every story has an obligatory or climactic scene that the narrative is heading toward. In this scene, which usually happens several minutes before the end of the film, all the conflict is resolved.

A Good Story Loves Contrast

If we deconstruct the screenplay backward from the climactic scene, we will notice that in one scene the hero moves closer to a positive climatic scene (the guy winning the girl's heart, for example) and in the next, he experiences a setback (the girl flirts with the guy's brother).

It's this contrast that keeps the audience on their toes and paying attention. It's as though the story works like this:

Scene one (+): Our hero really wants something.

Scene two (-): But the opportunity to get that something has been taken away.

Scene three (+): An opportunity arises that might help the hero get what they want.

Scene four (-): But that opportunity falls through.

Because these contrasting scenes have worked for centuries to captivate a human mind, let's use them to captivate people browsing our website.

Again, the simple use of contrast (positive and negative messaging) on our website will suffice, but directly writing the first three sections so they vacillate from positive to negative to positive is going to give your message a familiar and attractive flow.

What Value Will Your Customer Receive if They Do Business With You?

Not only will the inclusion of a value section contribute to the contrast you're inviting customers into, but it will also add a perceived value to your products and services.

For instance, if you're selling your customer a maintenance package when they buy an HVAC system for their home, you'd increase the perceived value of that maintenance package if you listed a few benefits:

▸ Never worry about your air conditioner breaking down.
▸ Never have to schedule maintenance again.
▸ Breathe cleaner air without having to change filters.

Where some companies would simply mention they have a maintenance package, this company is "adding perceived value" to that package by listing other benefits the package gets me.

If the maintenance package costs $200 per year, and I perceive that package as being accurately priced and truly worth about $200, then saying I never have to worry about it breaking down increases the perceived value to, let's say, $300. And never needing to schedule maintenance increases the perceived value to $350. Not only this, but breathing clean air all year is something I'd pay a premium for and so that raises the perceived value to something like $500.

Customers are much more likely to buy a $500 item if they can get it for only $200.

By using words, we just raised the perceived value of our products and gave our customer a much better deal.

How much would it cost you in overhead and supply to raise the value of your products by over 100 percent. You'd have to add a lot of gizmos and services to do that, right?

We just raised the value of our product by more than 100 percent simply by using words.

And words are free.

Tell Your Customer Everything They Get

For some customers, the bottom line question is What do I get in exchange for my hard-earned money?

In this section of the website, you're going to tell them.

- Can they save money?
- Can they save time?
- Will they reduce risk?
- Are they getting quality?
- Will this help them simplify life or avoid hassles?

If so, this section of the website should spell out the added value.

Be Specific. Be Visual.

The biggest mistake people make when it comes to writing their value proposition is they aren't specific enough.

If your product will help save your customer time or money, you want to say so. Avoid elusive language like "fulfilling" or "satisfied" and instead use specific language like "you'll save time this summer" or "your lawn will make your neighbors jealous."

It also helps to be visual. Of course the actual images you use in this section will help, but we can also use language that helps people "see, smell, and taste" the life they can experience.

"You'll come home to a clean, fresh house that will make you feel like the queen's own cleaning staff has come through your house." Or "You'll be wearing the tux you got married in within a few weeks!"

Can you see how this kind of language is more motivating than "Your house will be clean" or "You'll lose weight"?

Here is an example of how another company has illustrated the value it offers customers:

In the section below, list the value your products or service can deliver to a customer:

1. _____
2. _____
3. _____
4. _____
5. _____
6. _____
7. _____
8. _____

Include a Headline

Is there a common theme among all these problems? Is there one glaring header you could use to encapsulate the stakes?

Remember to always include a headline above each section. A website section without a headline is like a newspaper article without a headline. People will skip it.

Here are some example headlines that work great:

"Our customers no longer struggle with…"

"You don't have to be confused anymore."

"The stakes are high!"

"Act now and avoid the hassles."

"Our heart breaks when we see people struggle with…"

With a header and a list of problems you help people solve, you'll demonstrate both your understanding of your customers' problem and your compassionate desire to help them find resolution.

Now, sketch out what this section of your website could look like below.

Section 4: The Guide

Help your customer win at all costs. At StoryBrand we certify existing marketing agents in both our messaging framework and our Marketing Made Simple checklist. At the end of their training, our StoryBrand guides take an oath. One of the agreements of that oath is that they will "obsess over their customers' success." By this we mean that they will not simply try to get money out of their customers but rather provide an incredible return on their investment.

The day you stop losing sleep about your own success and start losing sleep over your customers' success is the day your business will start growing again.

Every hero needs a guide, and in this fourth section of the wireframed website, we're going to position ourselves as the guide.

Again, these sections can go in any order. Now that you've established the first three sections as a positive, negative, and then positive movement in the story, your customers are likely hooked.

Not only are they hooked on the story you're inviting them into, but because you've illustrated the stakes, they're in desperate need of help.

A Guide Is Empathetic and Authoritative

All good guides in a story exhibit two crucial characteristics. They understand the challenges their customers are experiencing and they have been able to solve those challenges for other people.

At StoryBrand we call this empathy and authority.

To position yourself as the guide your customer needs, you need to express empathy and demonstrate authority.

When we demonstrate empathy and authority, our customer instantly recognizes we are the person who can help them win the day.

The One-two Punch of Empathy and Authority

Together, empathy and authority make a powerful one-two punch.

Imagine if you went to a fitness trainer and told them that you were interested in losing twenty pounds, toning some muscle, and getting on a healthy eating plan. Maybe you even explain to the trainer some of the problems you've been facing with your diet and weight loss plan—specifically that you crave ice cream late at night and that you have a hard time staying motivated to do any kind of cardio workouts.

Now imagine two different potential responses from the trainer....

1. **In the first scenario,** the trainer tells you, "I feel your pain. I hate doing cardio too and could probably stand to lose ten pounds as well. Come to think of it, I also love ice cream. Maybe we should go get some together. I know this great place right down the street." *How likely would you be to pay this trainer any money?*

2. **In the second scenario,** the trainer takes his shirt off and shows you how he can make his six-pack dance. He tells you he doesn't eat crap like ice cream and launches into a spiel about how the latest research shows a diet of kale and cabbage is really the way to go, so you're just going to have to suck it up and get that temptation out of your house. *Again, how likely would you be to pay this trainer any money?*

Empathy without authority falls flat, as does authority without empathy.

But it's the guide who can empathize with your pain while also demonstrating a competency to get us out that we ultimately trust.

If the same trainer said to you, "I totally understand ice cream cravings. In fact, I used to really struggle with that too before I learned what I know now about regulating your blood sugar. I can teach you a plan I've used to help hundreds of guys just like you get in shape and feel really good about their bodies without losing all of the things they love about their life, ice cream included. And the cardio isn't bad. Twenty minutes at a time. You can do this."

That's the trainer you want to hire.

In this section of your website, you're going to clearly express empathy and demonstrate authority (or competency).

Here are a couple ways to communicate authority on your website:

- **Testimonials.** All testimonials aren't created equally— below we will discuss testimonies.
- **Logos of companies you've worked with.** This works especially well for B2B.
- **A simple statistic.** Talk about how many people you've helped, how many years you've been in business, or how many clients have worked with you.

Examples:

- This is why we've spent the last twenty years helping clients just like you get in shape.
- Join the 100,000+ who have already changed the way they sleep at night.
- With our collected 100+ years of experience in the industry.

You don't need much. Just a little authority does the trick. Here are a few ways to communicate empathy on your website:

- Mention their primary pain point. Few messages are more endearing than "We understand how it feels to struggle with…"
- Testimonials in which customers state how much you cared for them are powerful.
- Stating plainly "I feel your pain" helped Bill Clinton become president and will help you grow your business.

Empathy

How can you resonate with your clients' pain or problem?

We trust people who are like us, so you want to create a statement that shows you not only understand your customers' pain, but you have felt it. You have been there before or experienced it through previous customers.

Here's a trick: Complete this sentence: "we know what it feels like to _____ ."

Examples:

- ▶ We know what it feels like to be overlooked for a promotion.
- ▶ We know how frustrating it is to have a great looking website that doesn't result in sales.
- ▶ We know what it feels like to worry you're not doing the right thing.

Now It's Your Turn ⟶

What pain are your customers feeling? What problem is bothering them the most? And what single, short statement can you make to express the empathy you feel regarding their struggle? Feel free to use this section of the book as a rough draft and then transfer your results over to the paper wireframe you downloaded at MarketingMadeSimple.com to see it all come together.

_____

_____

_____

_____

Authority

How can you reassure your customer you have what it takes to help them solve their problem?

You don't need to brag about yourself, but you do need a few key items that illustrate that you have the ability to help solve your customer's problem because you have helped others.

When thinking through what type of authority you want to place on your website, make sure that the evidence of your authority directly relates to solving the problem your customer is facing. For instance, if you are a certified yoga instructor, but your business is lawn care, you do not want to put this on your website. This will confuse the customer. They will not have a category in their brains to put you in. Are you a yoga instructor or lawn care specialist? It would be better to put something like, "We've saved customers thousands of hours of working in their yards so they can spend more time enjoying it than working on it." Only put authority on your site that directly relates to their success.

In this next section we will walk through each type of authority and what to consider in choosing what goes on your website.

Don't Overdo the Authority

Be careful. If you communicate too much authority and not enough empathy, you will confuse your customer about who the story is about. Is it about you or them? Always make the story about them.

Express empathy and demonstrate authority through testimonials.

Including three or four customer testimonies on your website will greatly enhance your empathy and authority.

But most companies get testimonials wrong.

The main problem we see when our clients use testimonials is they are too long. And the second problem is they ramble.

When we train our StoryBrand certified guides, we ask them to listen for soundbites. We have them interview customers and report back to us on what they heard. Were there any soundbites that could be used to succinctly convince others to buy?

When collecting testimonials, you want to think of yourself as a news editor. If a television news station sends out a reporter to interview somebody on location, they likely come back with twenty minutes or more of footage. That footage is cut into soundbites that may last a few seconds. Why? Because not everything the interviewee says is actually interesting.

Here are a few different soundbites you can look for when collecting testimonials:

1. **Overcoming objections.** Look for (or ask for) testimonials that speak directly to a client overcoming the primary objections customers have about doing business with you. For example, "I worried this course was going to be a waste of time. I was wrong. I made more progress in six hours than I've made in ten years."

2. **Solving problems.** Look for (or ask for) testimonials that speak to a specific problem you helped a customer overcome. For example, "I'm on my feet all day at work, so by 5:00 p.m. my lower back is usually aching. I wore XYZ shoes for the first time, and by 5:00 p.m. I felt like I could do another shift without blinking. I haven't felt this good in ten years."

3. **Adding Value.** Look for (or ask for) testimonials that help clients pass the payment threshold by speaking to how much value they received. For example, "I was skeptical at first because of the price. But I can't tell you how glad I am I used XYZ lawn services instead of another company. I've never been so proud of my lawn."

■   ■   ■

Keep Testimonials Short

Once you have the right testimonial, make them short and scannable. You can even write them for your customer and then send the testimonials to them for approval. I'm not saying make something up or lie, I'm saying that you might have heard them tell you how you changed their life and you will know how to write it better than they do. Put a couple short sentences together and send it to them for approval.

Your customers are not writers. And they are not marketers. You may think you aren't a marketer either but even having read this far in your book, you know more than 90 percent of professional marketers out there.

Use a Head Shot

Consider using a head shot of the customers so the testimonials have an even greater personal appeal and are more believable and relatable.

People trust others who are willing to publicly stand behind their words.

Unless you've got NDAs to deal with, use your customer's name and image.

Now It's Your Turn

Collect a few testimonials for your site. Feel free to use this section of the book as a rough draft and then transfer your results over to the paper wireframe you downloaded at MarketingMadeSimple.com to see it all come together.

Testimonial #1:

_____
_____
_____
_____

Testimonial #2:

_____
_____
_____
_____

Testimonial #3:

_____
_____
_____
_____

Including Images of Customer Logos on Your Site Adds Authority

Another way to demonstrate authority is to include logos from B2B interactions, or even logos of press outlets in which you have been featured.

The great thing about including logos is it doesn't take up much room on a website and yet allows the person scanning your site to check off the "these people know what they're doing" line item in their brain.

At StoryBrand we often get the question "But will it work for me?" To overcome this objection we put logos from a variety of companies on our site. We change our website from time to time, but we have featured logos from nonprofits, small businesses, national and international brands, large companies, and small companies. We also have a section that says "StoryBrand Works for B2B and B2C Companies." Then we list all the different types of sectors that have gone through a StoryBrand workshop. This quickly gives authority while also overcoming a perceived objection that they're the only company StoryBrand won't work for.

You do not have to have logos on your website, but if you work with a variety of different customers this is a great space to answer the question "Do they work with companies like me?" Show a variety of logos to show the breadth of your work.

Now It's Your Turn

What logos will you include on your website? Feel free to use this section of the book as a rough draft and then transfer your results over to the paper wireframe you downloaded at MarketingMadeSimple.com to see it all come together.

Logos

_____

_____

_____

_____

Including Statistics Speaks to the Authority You Have
Statistics can be another great way to demonstrate your authority. The kinds of statistics you want to share should quickly and clearly let people know they can trust you to solve their problem.

Here are some examples of statistics that demonstrate your competency:

▶ Number of years helping people (number of years in business)
▶ Awards you've won
▶ Number of clients you've served
▶ Number of hours you've saved your clients
▶ Amount of money you've made your clients

Now It's Your Turn

What statistics will you include on your website? Feel free to use this section of the book as a rough draft and then transfer your results over to the paper wireframe you downloaded at MarketingMadeSimple .com to see it all come together.

_____

_____

_____

_____

Let's Put the Guide Section Together

We've given you plenty of examples for the guide section on your website. But remember, this section does not have to be long and involved.

You don't need to use each of these examples. If you don't have testimonials, don't worry. You can collect those and include them in the future. If you've not won awards, don't worry. All you need to do is quickly express empathy and quickly demonstrate authority and then move on. Never forget, you aren't telling a story about yourself here, you are inviting customers into a story. In that story, you play the guide, not the hero, so position yourself as the customers' guide and then get back to inviting them into a meaningful story.

Here is an example of how the guide section on your website can look:

Watch how this customer sold more with less work

Join thousands of businesses like yours that have sold over $350 million by using OrderMyGear.

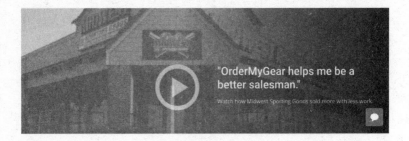

Now It's Your Turn

Sketch out a guide section for your website. Feel free to use this section of the book as a rough draft and then transfer your results over to the paper wireframe you downloaded at MarketingMadeSimple.com to see it all come together.

Section 5: The Plan

Pave a path for the customer and they will follow it. The plan section of your website tells customers what path they need to follow to do business with you.

By visually demonstrating what path your customers need to take, they see how easy it is to work with you and identify their next steps.

The reason we recommend a plan section is because people will not walk into a fog. If a customer is confused about what steps they need to take to buy your product or service, they will bounce from your site, using the excuse that they will come back later and figure it out. Of course we know they will not come back. They will likely never come back.

Although it may be obvious to you how a customer can buy your product or service, it is not obvious to them. Remember, customers are bombarded with commercial advertising and pitches every day and they will not spend mental bandwidth "figuring out the obvious," no matter how easy the obvious is to figure out.

When customers are thinking about buying, give them a few simple steps they can take to engage your brand and buy your products.

Comedian Brian Regan has a bit in his stand-up about looking at a box of Pop-Tarts and seeing directions on how to eat them. He mocks the simplicity of the instructions and how this should be obvious to anyone who has ever eaten anything.

Does anyone really need to know a three-step process to eat a Pop-Tart?

Of course not. But all comedy aside, the "plan" is on the side of the box as a way to communicate to the unconscious mind of the consumer that getting to a successful result is even simpler than they thought. The visual representation of three steps, open the Pop-Tart package, warm the Pop-Tart, and then eat the Pop-Tart, actually says, "This is going to be easy. You're going to have some sugar running through your veins in just a few minutes!" And that simple message translates into sales.

When you add a plan section to your website, it's as though you're saying to your customer, "It's impossible to mess this up."

Using Three Steps Is the Key

We recommend a three-step plan. You can use four if you like, but don't go much past four. The more steps you have in your plan, the more complicated it looks visually and the less a customer will be willing to take the journey.

The reality is there may be seven or eight steps a customer needs to take to do business with you, but do yourself a favor and combine some of those steps into three phases. Having three steps keeps things simple and easy.

If you're shopping for a caterer for an upcoming party, for example, you'll be more likely to do business with a company that breaks down their process into three steps:

1. Tell us about your event.
2. Let us create a custom menu.
3. Host the party of your dreams.

Imagine searching for a caterer and their website simply said, "We will be your favorite, caterer, we promise," but didn't spell out a simple plan. Likely, you'd feel a little tension and confusion about how the process would work. Hiring a caterer and getting all that food to your house is involved, and because you don't know how it works, you are more likely to pass in favor of a business in which you better understand the process.

Keep the Plan Visually Simple

You'll want each step of your plan to be represented by a word or simple phrase. Remember, people scan websites before they read them so make your website easy to scan by putting key words in bold text or using bullet points for easy reading.

You can also use icons for each step, bolded headers, and short descriptions so the visitor doesn't have to burn very many mental calories to figure out how you're going to lead them to their successful result.

Exercise

Can doing business with you be broken down into three steps? What would those steps be? For instance, 1. Call 2. Plan 3. Build.

Below, write your three step process plan—how are you going to lead your customers to a successful result?

1. _____

2. _____

3. _____

Now that you have the words that represent each step, you can use a sentence or two underneath the headers to further describe each step. In these short sentences talk about the benefits the customer will see if they take these steps or share any information that will make the process more clear.

For instance, if step one in the plan is to "set up a call," what benefits will they receive from that call? Will it save them time, will they find out if they're a good fit, will they get information they currently don't have? If step two in the plan is to "get a plan," will they stop wasting time, will they get your expert advice, with they have a clear path forward?

Each step of the plan should have a few words that discuss the benefits for the customer. Take a minute and brainstorm what benefits the client will get when they take each step?

1. SCHEDULE A MEETING
Meet with Tyler so he can get to know you and help define where you want to go

2. CREATE A PLAN
Together we'll create a specific plan to accomplish your goals

3. GET RESULTS
Succeed stress-free in Seattle's competitive housing market

Step 1 benefits.

_____

_____

_____

_____

Step 2 benefits.

_____

_____

_____

_____

Step 3 benefits.

_____

_____

_____

_____

Now put it all together. Sketch out below what the plan section of your website should look like. Use icons or numbers to represent the steps in the plan and then put the short descriptors underneath.

Now It's Your Turn ————————————————→

Sketch out a plan section for your website. Feel free to use this section of the book as a rough draft and then transfer your results over to the paper wireframe you downloaded at MarketingMadeSimple.com to see it all come together.

Section 6: The Explanatory Paragraph

We often hear from clients who worry that trimming their text to make it pass the "grunt test" means they won't be able to answer all of their client's questions, provide them with the necessary information—especially for products or services that are more complicated—or communicate everything they believe their clients need to know to do business with them.

As the landing page or website gets deeper, though, you can use more and more text.

Most people bounce from a website because there are too many useless words at the top. By designing your website the way we've recommended, your customer is already hooked. Because you've told them what you offer, how it can make their lives better, and what they need to do to buy it, we can further elaborate on your offer because your potential customers are willing to give us a little more time.

The Explanatory Paragraph
Is Where Your SEO Will Come From

If you are worried about search engine optimization (SEO) on your website, the explanatory paragraph is going to ease your fears. While SEO algorithms change often, simply including long-form text using words that sell your products is going to help.

In addition, including a long-form explanatory paragraph allows customers to feel like they've done due diligence in researching whether or not to buy your product or service.

Most people don't like to buy impulsively. They have a healthy regulator in their brain that wants to check off a few boxes that make them feel as though they've done a little research. For most potential customers, your explanatory paragraph will scratch that itch.

Still, the explanatory paragraph is easy to mess up. If you ramble on and on about the history of the company and how proud you are of your accomplishments, you'll waste your customers' time.

What your customer really wants is to be invited into a story. And your explanatory paragraph is going to accomplish exactly that.

Invite Customers Into a Story

If you've read my book *Building a StoryBrand,* you already know how to invite customers into a story. But if you haven't, don't worry. I'm going to share a quick and easy formula with you that will make the writing easy. I recommend following this formula word for word for your first pass, then nuancing it so that it feels true to your voice.

Your explanatory paragraph is going to do the following:

1. Identify who your customer wants to become.
2. Identify what they want.
3. Define the problem setting them back.
4. Position you as their guide.
5. Share a plan they can use to solve their problem (which includes your product).
6. Call them to action.
7. Cast a vision for their lives.

This magical paragraph is essentially a story your potential customers can lean into. And they will feel that as they read it.

Let's look at the paragraph Mad Lib–style, then I'll slowly explain each piece so you can fill it out on your own.

■   ■   ■

A Sample Explanatory Paragraph ⟶

At _____ [your company name] we know you are the kind of people who want to be _____ [aspirational identity. What kind of person do they want to become?]. In order to be that way, you need _____ [As it relates to your product, what does your customer want?]. The problem is _____ [What's the physical problem holding them back?], which makes you feel _____ [How is that problem making them feel?]. We believe _____ [Why is it just plain wrong that anybody should have to deal with that problem?]. We understand _____ [Include an empathetic statement]. That's why we _____ [Demonstrate your competency to solve their problem]. Here's how it works _____ [What's your three-step plan: step one, step two, step three]. So _____ [Call them to action], so you can stop _____ [What negative thing will happen or continue to happen if they don't order?] and start _____ [What will their life look like if they do place an order?].

Write and rewrite your explanatory paragraph until it is smooth and makes sense. You'll notice that what you've really done with this paragraph is created a mental map for your customer. After reading this paragraph, they suddenly know what's been troubling them, how to overcome whatever has been troubling them, and what steps they need to take to move forward. Their world, as it relates to your product and service, now makes sense.

And remember, people move toward clarity and away from confusion.

I've had many, many clients tell me they went to my website and decided to make a purchase after reading the explanatory paragraph. What they're really telling me is that they placed an order once my product started making sense and only after they felt like they'd done due diligence.

The explanatory paragraph is a great way to accomplish both.

Another Option for the Explanatory Paragraph: Overcome Your Client's Objections

Another way to write your explanatory paragraph is to overcome customer objections.

Every potential customer who comes to your website has questions or fears about doing business with you. Your explanatory paragraph is an opportunity to overcome those fears and remove any hurdles that would keep them from doing business with you. Sometimes just overcoming one objection can lead to a sale.

To do this, you want to start by listing the top five reasons why someone would *not* want to do business with you.

What are the five excuses or questions you hear from customers who are unwilling to place an order?

These questions could be:

- The product is too expensive.
- I doubt it will work for me.
- What happens if it doesn't work for me?
- I doubt the quality is as good as they're saying it is.
- The process is going to take too long.
- I won't know how to use it once I place an order.
- I've tried something like this and it didn't work.

After you have listed the top five excuses, craft a sentence or two that overcomes each objection. For example, if the question is "Is the process complicated?" you could write a sentence that says, "We guide you through an *easy* process to help you use our product so you never have to worry about X again."

If the question is "What happens if I'm not satisfied?" you could write "we have a 100 percent satisfaction money-back guarantee."

Once you have those sentences written out, turn them into a paragraph that can go on your website.

Below, list the top five reasons why someone would not want to do business with you, followed by your response to overcome this objection.

Reason #1 _____
_____
_____
_____

Response #1 _____
_____
_____
_____

Reason #2 _____
_____
_____
_____

Response #2 _____
_____
_____
_____

Reason #3 _____
_____
_____
_____

Response #3 _____

_____

_____

_____

Reason #4 _____

_____

_____

_____

Response #4 _____

_____

_____

_____

Reason #5 _____

_____

_____

_____

Response #5 _____

_____

_____

_____

If you'd like to use both examples of explanatory paragraphs, feel free. Your customers can continue scrolling down your landing page forever. No landing page is too long, as long as the text and images are interesting. If you do use both explanatory paragraphs, just make sure to separate them by a few sections so your landing page doesn't look like it contains too much text. When a customer sees a lot of text, they start thinking you're going to make them work too hard to buy your product and they're more likely to bounce. Never forget, your customer wants the process of buying and receiving your product to be easy. So even with these long-form paragraphs, don't waste words.

Now It's Your Turn →

Write your explanatory paragraph (one or both types) in the space provided. Feel free to use this section of the book as a rough draft and then transfer your results to the paper wireframe you downloaded at MarketingMadeSimple.com to see it all come together.

Section 7: The Video

This is another opportunity to present your sales pitch. The next section of your website is where you will include the video. While you don't have to include a video, we recommend creating one that repeats your message narratively and visually.

Many potential customers will simply scroll down to the video section without reading much of anything. For this reason, your video simply needs to repeat what's already been said.

And even if they do read your page word for word, repeating those words in your video goes a long way in helping them memorize your offer.

Creating video does not have to be complicated. In fact, if you simply read your explanatory paragraph into a microphone and lay that text over "B-roll" of people using your product, you should be fine.

If you'd like to get a little more advanced, consider elaborating on your explanatory paragraph with customer testimonials or even a message from your CEO.

If you're going to include a video, though, here are some rules we recommend following.

- ▶ **Keep it short.** Most experts say a commercial video on a website shouldn't extend much beyond three minutes. I agree with that as a general rule, but of course if a video is interesting, it can go for five minutes or more. That said, though, I've rarely seen a five-minute video that couldn't have been trimmed down.
- ▶ **Hook the viewer:** One study shows that 33 percent of viewers click away and move on after the first thirty seconds of a web video. Ensure you grab the viewer's attention quickly. How? Make sure the first thing the viewer hears and sees is a problem. What problem do

you solve for your customer? State it right out of the gate and move on from there.

- **Consider giving a longer video away in exchange for an email:** If a potential customer has given you their email address in exchange for watching a video, they will actually watch a great deal longer? Why? Because they've "invested" something and will take the video more seriously. If you have a longer video, like a fifteen- or twenty-minute TED talk, with useful and engaging information, consider giving it away in exchange for an email as a lead generator. That said, don't post the entire video on your homepage. Create a separate landing page to deliver the longer video.
- **Give your video a title.** Many people simply post a YouTube link on their homepage and check the "video" box off their website to-do list. This is a mistake. Actually give your video a title that makes people want to watch it and then place that title in bold text above the play button for that video. You'll find that the number of plays increases dramatically. Consider titles like "How we've helped thousands solve X problem" or "Here's how our process is different."

The general rule here is that your video should be a sales pitch. It should help you close the deal. Don't make the mistake of being vague and elusive in your video, turning it into some sort of brand identity art installation. Your customer wants to hear your pitch in a concise, clear, and interesting form, and your video is a great opportunity to accomplish this.

—— *Now It's Your Turn* ————————————→

What will your video be called? What narration do you want over your video? What do you need to shoot in order to create a video? Write some thoughts below and consider creating a video an important project over the next few months. Feel free to use this section of the book as a rough draft and then transfer your results over to the paper wireframe you downloaded at MarketingMadeSimple.com to see it all come together.

Notes on Creating a Video:

_____

_____

_____

_____

Section 8: Price Choices

Let's get to the bottom line. Many clients either have custom pricing or too many products to list prices on their website. Don't feel like you have to list your prices.

But, if you're working with products with a fixed cost, and you are willing to put those on your site, spell out the cost followed by bullet points of what the customer gets with each price point.

Also, if a customer clicks on one of the prices or products, that link should go to a page only talking about that specific product. To create that landing page, simply follow the exact same formula you've used on the main landing page, only make the text and images specific to that product.

In this way, you can have a complex tree of links and websites but continue using this clear methodology so that your customer never feels confused or lost.

When listing the prices of your products, we recommend having three different options. Even if you only have one product, consider packaging other items or services with that product so you can have three different price points. Why? Because customers like having options, and when you give them a few options, they are more likely to choose and purchase one.

If you are selling many products, simply list your bestselling products on your landing page here and then move into a more catalog-style layout when customers click "shop." Or perhaps include divisions of your offering like "Men," "Women," and "Children," and then use the three-price-point option on each product when you create those separate landing pages.

Speaking of three price points, many of our StoryBrand certified marketing guides have discovered that customers usually choose to buy the item featured in the middle. They don't want the cheapest or the most expensive, but they do want good value.

Again, make sure to spell out what customers get with each price point and you'll have much more success.

Here is an example of simple price options laid out on a website:

DOG FOOD

Memphis Barbeque Slow Cooked Stew Wet Dog Food
$3.74

Wild Kangaroo Entree Wet Dog Food
$5.99

Lamb Entree Wet Dog Food
$4.39

Duck Stew Wet Dog Food
$3.74

Now It's Your Turn

What will the pricing section of your website look like? Feel free to use this section of the book as a rough draft and then transfer your results over to the paper wireframe you downloaded at MarketingMadeSimple .com to see it all come together.

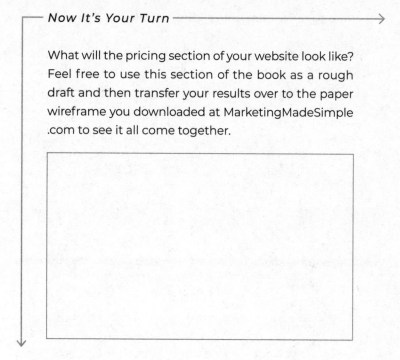

Section 9: Junk Drawer

The most important section of your website. Because it's where you're going to put everything you previously thought was important!

Many websites feature too many buttons and options at the top of the page. We strongly recommend putting most of these options at the bottom of the website in what we call the junk drawer.

The reason you don't want too many links at the top of the page is because you'll cause a potential customer to experience decision fatigue. The most important links are for your direct call to action and your transitional call to action, which I'll cover in the next chapter.

People will scroll to the bottom to find a link to employment opportunities, contact info, and even "about us," so reserve the top of the page for those who aren't yet committed to giving you much time.

Simply move the contact, FAQ, about, employment opportunities, and so forth to the bottom of the page so that if people want to find them, they can. Use your junk drawer to clean up the clutter!

Exercise ————————————————————————→

What are you going to include in your Junk Drawer?

_____

_____

_____

_____

Sketch out everything you will feature in your junk drawer. Feel free to use this section of the book as a rough draft and then transfer your results over to the paper wireframe you downloaded at Marketing MadeSimple.com to see it all come together.

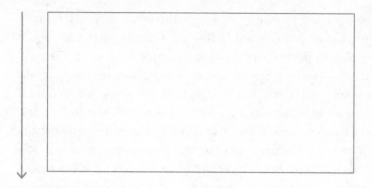

LET'S PUT TOGETHER A WEBSITE THAT WORKS

While there can be many other sections on a website, these nine sections are the ones we consider to be critical. Hundreds of guides helping tens of thousands of businesses create websites that work can't be wrong. If it works for other businesses like yours, it will work for you.

Now that you have all the different sections created you can lay them out in a way that feels right for you.

Use the sales funnel wireframe you downloaded at Marketing-MadeSimple.com to wireframe your new website.

While there are many digital tools that allow you to create websites, I recommend using paper and pen to write all the text. Why? Because by handwriting the text you're paying a great deal more attention to what you are saying and how many words you're using. You also aren't getting distracted by digital images that may look pretty but sell nothing.

In addition, wireframing a website on paper takes time. It's a slower process, and you're more likely to meditate on what you're presenting. That time and focus is going to translate into increased sales.

Not only will you have spent more thoughtful time wireframing your website, but if you do bring your site to a designer, you'll have already done the majority of the work.

If you're using a StoryBrand certified guide, they will already know why you've laid out your website the way you have, but if you're using somebody who isn't familiar with our framework, don't let them talk you out of wireframing your website using these exact tools. Again, we've proven that these sections of a website work terrifically to create and increase sales. Don't be fooled by mood boards and motion graphics. This website framework will work!

After you wireframe your website, you will have completed the first two components of your sales funnel. You now have a one-liner and a wireframed website.

But that's just the beginning. The real key to increasing sales is the process of collecting email addresses and sending out emails and sales scripts. That process leads to orders in an automated system.

Let's move on to the third component of our sales funnel: the lead generator.

6

LEAD GENERATOR

*Give Them a Reason to Give You
Their Email Address or They Won't*

Imagine meeting somebody you find interesting but not exchanging contact information. Unless you happen to meet again somewhere, you're likely to forget about that person in a short period of time.

But sometimes those first encounters are awkward. It doesn't feel quite right to ask for contact information or to give it out uninvited.

In business relationships, lead generators are a great excuse to exchange contact information without being awkward. Think of the exchange going something like this: "Hey, let me send you that information I was talking about. What's your email address?"

Lead generators that capture emails make sure that when someone finds you interesting you are getting their contact info. Stop missing out on the opportunity to *get those digits!*

PEOPLE WANT TO STAY IN TOUCH WITH YOU IF YOU ARE INTERESTING AND CAN HELP THEM SURVIVE

Now that you have a one-liner and website, your potential customer is curious about how you can help them solve their problem and they want more information.

Now that you've earned the right to be heard, they will be willing to spend more time with you. A good lead-generating PDF should take about twenty minutes to read, which, while it doesn't sound like much, is actually quite a commitment from any customer.

Congratulations. Because you've piqued your customers' curiosity and positioned yourself as the guide, they're willing to put skin in the game.

You're officially in a committed relationship.

Think of the one-liner as the first introduction to somebody and your website as the first, second, and third date. Your lead generator, then, is going to be the first time your customer actually commits.

Of course it's not time yet for a financial commitment, but when they gave you their email address, they definitely entered into a healthy business transaction with you.

While giving you their email address is not a financial commitment, don't be fooled. It's still a very big commitment.

Most people do not part with their email address easily. For a potential customer, parting with their email address is the equivalent of them giving you a ten or twenty dollar bill. They don't want to receive junk mail or spam and they don't want their email box to be cluttered with trash, so they give out their address sparingly.

In fact, most people don't want to give out their email address at all, and fewer and fewer people are willing to do it. Still, that's good news for you. Why? There is one reason: anybody who is willing to give you an email address is very interested in your product or service.

The more culture changes and the less people want to give you their email address, the better the lead they actually are.

How do we get somebody to give us their email address? We give them great value in return and we honor their inbox.

FREE VALUE LEADS TO TRUST

A lead generator is (usually) a free asset you offer potential clients as a way of building authority and trust.

Your lead generator can be a PDF, a video series, a free sample, a live event, or anything you can give your potential customer that helps them solve a problem.

We recommend starting with a lead-generating PDF.

StoryBrand, the marketing and messaging division of Business Made Simple, was built using a single PDF called "The Five Things Your Website Should Include." This simple PDF was downloaded by thousands of people, and hundreds of them ended up coming to our live marketing workshops. Without that PDF, we'd have never gotten off the ground.

From that PDF, we created more sales funnels that offered more PDFs, and then we added free video courses and webinars and even free live teaching events. Soon, we were collecting hundreds of email addresses each day and our business started to grow quickly.

The great thing about starting with a lead-generating PDF is that they are cheap to create. Unlike the old days where you'd have to print a book, a lead generator can be short, visual, compelling, and helpful and yet can be created and designed in a weekend.

Lead generators should position you as the customers' guide, answer your clients' questions, solve their problems, pique their interest, stir a sense of reciprocity, build trust in what you have to offer, challenge a potential customer to take small action, give them a vision of the successful result they could experience, and ultimately *lead* them to a nurture campaign, a sales campaign, and hopefully a sale.

WHAT SHOULD A LEAD GENERATOR ACCOMPLISH?

A great lead generator should do the following things:

1. **Position yourself as the guide.** This is an opportunity to share empathy and authority with your potential customer. Show how you are the right guide to help them solve their problem.
2. **Stake claim to your territory.** Take this opportunity to differentiate from the crowd. Share your unique knowledge on a subject and demonstrate how you can solve the customer's problem.
3. **Qualify your audience.** Your lead generator should speak to the specific audience you are trying to reach. If there are varying segments of people you're reaching out to, you can create different lead generators to reach those different audiences. For instance, if you are a financial advisor who works with different types of clients, target those specific audiences. If one audience you are targeting is just getting started in investing, you can offer a lead generator titled "Five mistakes people make with their first investment." If you are targeting a demographic that is further along in the process you can offer a lead generator titled "How to pass on your money without spoiling your children." These will be downloaded by different demographics of people. Then you can create email campaigns that market to each specifically.

4. **Create trust by solving a problem.** We keep saying it over and over, so you should notice that it's important. The purpose of any business is to solve somebody's problem. Unless you talk about that problem, nobody will know why you exist. But even though your product solves a problem, your lead generator should also solve a problem. For free. Once you start solving your customers' problems, they will trust you with more of their problems. For instance, you can share nutritional tips for eating organic in your lead generator and then invite people to classes teaching them to grow a backyard garden. Some marketing experts say it this way "Give away the why but sell the how." I like that rule, but I also like giving away some of the how just to be generous. At StoryBrand we give more away in our podcast—Business Made Simple daily advice videos and lead-generators—than most universities sell in their MBA programs. But that's okay. I don't think it has cost us a thing. I've never been punished for being generous, and besides, not everybody has the money. But that doesn't mean they don't deserve a place at the table. Be kind and generous to your customers and they will remember you when they are successful.

5. **Create reciprocity.** When you give value for free, customers feel indebted to you and to your brand—even if it's not conscious. When you give away great content and value, customers want to return the favor and are more likely to place orders.

6. **Have an interesting title.** Make sure to use a title people will want to download. Nobody wants to download a "white paper" or "case study," but they do want to download "The five mistakes most people make when training a puppy" or "How Nancy doubled her revenue without leaving the house." Make your title catchy and bold.

WHAT KIND OF LEAD-GENERATING PDFS CAN YOU CREATE?

Lead-generating PDF's do not have to be complicated. Again, you should be able to create an effective lead generator in a long weekend. The key is not to overthink it.

The reality is, in your industry, you're likely an expert. And if you aren't an expert, you certainly know a lot more about whatever products you represent than your potential customers. By sharing some of that knowledge, you position yourself as their guide. And that's half the battle.

Let's look at ten ideas for PDFs that will be easy to create and offer terrific value to customers:

1. Capture an Interview With an Industry Expert

A great way to establish your authority and stake claim to your territory is to interview an expert with an intricate knowledge of your industry.

If you work within a specific niche, find an influencer and schedule some time to meet with that person. Ask questions that you know your customers are asking and guide the interviewee toward answers that contain practical knowledge that solve real problems.

For example, a pet shelter might sit down with their head of adoption and ask: "What are the seven things every family should consider before adopting a puppy?"

If you do marketing for a tax firm, interview a CPA and ask: "Tell me the five biggest mistakes people make when they do their own taxes."

This interview isn't just limited to a PDF, by the way. You can distribute the conversation via live webinar, audio recording, podcast, or PDF article.

Exercise ⟶

Who are three people you could interview who would provide exceptional value for your customers?

_____

_____

_____

_____

2. Checklist

A checklist is a great place to start if you want to try a lead-generating content strategy but don't have a lot of time.

A checklist is simple. It walks your readers through a list of ideas to consider related to solving their problem.

Let's say you run a health clinic. Your checklist could ask a series of health questions, such as:

"Do you get winded walking up the stairs?"

"Do you feel tired every day around 3:00 p.m.?"

"Do you ever have trouble sleeping at night?"

With each question, you can highlight the ways that your clinic can help them solve the problem they've identified.

If you sell cookware and kitchen supplies, your checklist might be built around the "fifty items every well-stocked pantry needs."

A checklist is often a great way to make customers aware of what they're lacking—and how you can help.

If you sell intellectual property or training, consider a checklist that informs your customer about how to become better at whatever rests in your area of expertise. If you're a speaking coach, think about a PDF called "Ten terrific ways to start a speech" or "Three things that make a speaker look like an amateur." Anybody interested in growing their speaking ability is undoubtedly going to download that checklist.

Exercise

What are some checklists you can create to help your customer realize they are missing the product you have?

_____

_____

_____

_____

3. Make a Worksheet Your Audience Will Use Over and Over

Think of an area in your clients' lives that you can help facilitate, and create a repeatable worksheet that solves their problem.

A worksheet could be anything from a weekly marketing planner to a goal-setting page.

Daily or weekly worksheets might take something overwhelming and make it simple.

Have the worksheet be something they can use repeatedly so they're reminded weekly or even daily that you exist and can help them.

Worksheet ideas can be anything from nutrition journals, homework schedulers, lawn maintenance journals, birthday reminders, to any other area in which a person might need to organize their thoughts.

Exercise ⟶

What are three areas in which your customers could use help organizing their thoughts and you could create a worksheet to help?

_____

_____

_____

_____

4. Host an Educational Event

Educational events aren't always gimmicky. They can be extremely valuable if the offer helps your customers solve a problem.

A giveaway can also remind people what it is you offer. A free cooking class for a local catering company is a terrific idea. A seminar on how to save and buy your first home could be great for a mortgage company.

People are often hungry for more information before they are willing to buy. If you offer that information, they're more likely to buy from you!

Exercise ⟶

What kinds of educational events could you host that might build trust with your customers?

_____

_____

_____

_____

5. The Sampler

Depending on the kind of products and services you offer, you may be able to give away a sample to your potential customers.

For example, if you're selling an annual planner, you could feature a PDF about effective time management along with seven days of worksheets to fill out. This way, your lead receives something of value, but you've also created an opportunity to sell them on the annual planner.

If you have a food product or specialty product, see if there is a sample you can give away. Grocery stores give away samples for a reason. Samples lead to sales!

Other examples could be dinner recipes, cocktail recipes, a stylebook of new hairstyles, one free lawn mowing coupon, a free makeover, or even a free meal.

If you have a physical location, you can offer a coupon that is redeemable by coming into the store.

Exercise →

What is something small you can give away to build trust with your potential customers and introduce them to the quality of your product or service?

_____

_____

_____

_____

6. Webinars

Webinars are a great way to engage your customers.

The goal of a webinar should be to offer training or information that will help your customer overcome a specific problem.

Your customers will attend the webinar for free—in exchange for their email address—and at the end of the webinar, you not only have the opportunity to make an offer for a paid product, you are also able to follow up with a nurture or sales campaign in the weeks and months that follow.

After the webinar is concluded, you can also take the exact same information you shared and turn it into a lead-generating PDF that is downloadable from your website.

Exercise

What are some topics you might be able to cover in a webinar?

_____

_____

_____

_____

7. Develop a Keynote Presentation Into a Lead-Generating Event

Delivering a keynote is an excellent way to generate demand for your services.

No matter what type of product or service you offer, find an area where you are an expert and create a speech you can deliver at events. You might even be able to create your own event and invite the public.

Creating talks like "Five mistakes accountants make that are costing you money" or "Get the most out of your team without killing them" will attract customers that likely need your respective products or services.

If you are B2C, find interesting facts or information that people don't know. If you sell shoes, consider a talk called "Couch to 5k is easier than you think" or "How your shoes could be making you feel lazy!"

Exercise →

What are three areas of expertise that you could turn into keynote presentations that position you as an expert?

_____

_____

_____

_____

8. Scratch the Curiosity Itch

We've all lost precious time by clicking on a link just because we were curious. What do those childhood celebrities look like now? How did they build the world's biggest boat?

Without knowing it, by clicking on these clickbait titles we've lost five minutes of our lives we will likely never get back. But you have to admit they are kind of fun.

Once, while working with a global pet food brand, I recommended they turn their network of dog parks into lead generators. The company was incredibly generous to create dog parks all over the world, but none of them were being used as lead generators. My recommendation? Create a lead generator called "Five things your dog thinks about at a dog park" and allow people to download it to their phones. After all, most dog owners just stand around looking at their phones anyway. Might as well tell them why all those dogs are sniffing each other's rears!

Exercise →

What are your potential customers curious about as it relates to your product or service and how could you turn that curiosity into a lead generator?

_____

_____

_____

_____

9. Pitfall List

Much like the checklist, there are pitfalls and challenges that your potential customer is experiencing you can help them avoid.

Titles like "Five money mistakes to avoid making when buying a house" or "Three fatal mistakes managers make when coaching their teams" or "Ten interview blunders that will ensure you don't get the job" help potential customers avoid pain and help you earn their trust as an expert.

■   ■   ■

What are three titles that would represent lists of pitfalls you can help customers avoid?

_____

_____

_____

_____

10. Open House

You might be surprised to learn that open houses have nothing to do with selling that specific house and everything to do with the real estate agent building a relationship with potential clients.

For our real estate clients, open houses are a tremendous way to capture contact information and lead them into a nurture campaign where you begin solving problems.

An open house doesn't have to just be for real estate agents, though. Offering a free product demonstration, cooking classes, craft nights, inviting people over to your home to hear about what you do, all create a sense of community and build relationships.

Exercise →

What's a good reason to invite people into your home or business to hear a pitch? What types of events could you host that might bring potential clients together?

_____

_____

_____

_____

NEVER STOP THINKING OF LEAD GENERATORS

Most people hate to sell, and one of the great thing about lead generators is it gives you an excuse to talk about your products and services without asking for money. If somebody downloads your lead generator or shows up to hear your speech, they want to know more, and it makes the sales conversation that comes later much more natural and authentic.

Never stop thinking about lead generators. You should probably spend about as much time thinking of lead generators as you do creating products. Why? Because without them you probably aren't going to sell many products anyway.

I hope these ideas have been helpful.

With a lead generator, you'll attract the kind of customers who really need and want the service you have to offer, you'll dramatically grow your email list, and you'll be able to close sales in a natural, nonsleazy way.

NOW LET'S MAKE YOUR LEAD-GENERATING PDF: HERE'S A STEP-BY-STEP GUIDE

Create Your Captivating Title

The first thing to consider is the title of your PDF. Again, you want it to be catchy and strong. Give people a reason to download the PDF by showing the value you're offering right there in the title.

Here are some sample PDF titles that have been well received:

Five mistakes people make with their first million dollars. A downloadable PDF guide offered by a financial advisor who wanted to identify young, newly wealthy clients.

Building your dream home: Ten things to get right before you build. A free e-book offered by an architect who wanted to establish herself as a guide to families looking to build a custom home.

Cocktail club: Learn to make one new cocktail each month. This was a monthly event put on (surprisingly) by a garden center. They taught attendees how to infuse alcohol with herbs. The objective for the promotion was to create community and to educate people about how to grow an herb garden. Did it work? Business is booming—or should I say blooming!

How to become a professional speaker. A free online course offered by a business coach for those who wanted to become professional speakers. This generated leads for long-term subscriptions to his coaching service.

How to get your dog to stop barking when people knock at the door. This was offered by a pet store and helped establish them as an expert in dog training and pet care.

Five surprising aches and pains caused by your shoes (and how to fix them). A pitfall list offered by an athletic wear store to highlight how cheap shoes are not worth the low cost.

Five mistakes most managers make that are squashing productivity (I bet you did number three this morning). Another pitfall list offered by a management consultant.

Now that you've considered your title, let's move on to the meat of the PDF. Remember, you do not have to use a great deal of text. You simply need to solve your customer's problem and earn trust in the new relationship.

Content: The Meat in the Middle

There are a million ways to write a PDF, but I'm going to give you a little formula that will make it easy.

If you aren't a professional writer, don't worry. All you need to do is create a little outline and hire a copywriter to flesh it out.

Believe me, this little outline is going to make the copywriter's job much more easy, and the end product will be terrific.

Here we go:

Catchy Title: _____

Section 1:

Paragraph 1: What's a problem your customers are experiencing?

Paragraph 2: What is an empathetic statement you can make about their pain? And what have you accomplished that would elicit trust that you can solve their problem?

Section 2:

Paragraph 1: Agitate the problem a little further. Speak, perhaps, to the emotional frustration a person may experience when dealing with the challenge you help solve.

Paragraph 2: Offer a solution to the problem. Three tips, a paradigm shift, a recipe or formula, something that resolves the conflict for your customer.

Section 3:

Spell out the solution in a step-by-step plan or in a list of tips. Offer the five tips, expert advice, or worksheet that can help your customers overcome their problem. This is the main content of the PDF.

Step/Tip 1 _____

Step/Tip 2 _____

Step/Tip 3 _____

Section 4: (Define the stakes)

What's at stake if they do or don't heed your advice? What will be won or lost if they don't take action on what you've recommended?

Paragraph 1: List the negative consequences that might happen if they don't act on your advice followed by the happy ending they may receive if they do.

Paragraph 2: Call them to action. What should they do next?

This is a basic template for creating a lead-generating PDF, but it works quite well.

Here is the actual text from a lead-generating PDF we created for a fake e-bike company. We used this very template:

10 WAYS AN
E-BIKE WILL
MAKE AND
SAVE YOU
MONEY

DOWNLOAD OUR FREE PDF AND START
DOWN THE ROAD TO SAVING MONEY

DOWNLOAD THE PDF

Now It's Your Turn ⟶

Create the four sections that will give you the foundation you need to create a great lead-generating PDF.
Feel free to use this section of the book as a rough
draft and then transfer your results over to the
lead-generating PDF outline you downloaded at Mar-
ketingMadeSimple.com. Work with your designer or
visit MarketingMadeSimple.com to hire a certified
StoryBrand guide who can create a PDF for you.

Catchy Title: _____

Section 1:

Paragraph 1: (Problem)

_____
_____
_____
_____

Paragraph 2: (Empathetic statement and elicit trust)

_____

_____

_____

_____

Section 2:

Paragraph 1: (Agitate the problem)

_____

_____

_____

_____

Paragraph 2: (Offer a solution)

_____

_____

_____

_____

Section 3: (Step-by step plan or list of tips)

_____

_____

_____

_____

Section 4:

Paragraph 1: (Negative consequences if they don't act
and include a happy ending if they do)

_____

_____

_____

_____

Paragraph 2: (Call them to action)

_____

_____

_____

_____

WHAT DO YOU DO WITH YOUR LEAD GENERATOR?

Once you have your lead generator created, the first thing you want to do is promote it on your website. You can create a section on your website to advertise it, but I also recommend a pop-up ad.

Yes, I know, pop-up ads are annoying, but they work. They typically have a higher click rate than regular ads and are an effective way of capturing potential customers' emails before they leave your site.

A few tips for pop-up ads:

1. **Give the visitor time to browse.** Don't make the pop-up ad show up immediately. Give them around ten seconds on the website before bringing up the ad. You can also create an "intent to exit" pop-up. This type of pop-up ad only comes up when the visitor moves their mouse to click off your site. This allows users to browse without being interrupted but still works to capture information before they leave.
2. **Know the rules.** Search engines are constantly changing the rules about how you can use pop-ups. You can be penalized for them being too big and covering too much of the site. Because the rules are changing all the time, we recommend talking to a professional or doing the research first before designing your ad.

3. **Don't let them close the ad with an X.** It has become second nature for most of us to close ads as soon as they pop up by hitting the X in the top right hand corner without even reading the ad. Instead, make your website visitor click on a sentence to close out the ad. The sentence can say something like, "No thanks, I don't want to save money" or something even stronger like "I'm okay letting the competition win." This might feel like clickbait, but it forces them to actually read what you are offering before opting out.

PROMOTE YOUR LEAD GENERATOR

We actually spend more advertising dollars promoting our lead generators than our products. They are that effective at leading to sales.

Consider promoting your lead generators on social media or even using paid advertising.

To promote our lead generators, we include ads for them on our websites, but we also create separate landing pages that focus on each lead generator exclusively. This way, we can link to specific pages in specific posts, ads, or podcast episodes.

The landing pages don't need to look exactly like your homepage, but make sure the copy on each page adheres to your brand's StoryBrand messaging principles or you'll risk confusing your customers. Keep the text clear, easy to understand, and punchy.

TIPS ON GOOD WRITING

As I mentioned before, you can be very creative with lead-generators, but the simplest and most cost effective is a lead-generating PDF.

Before you begin the writing process, keep in mind a few common mistakes clients make when it comes to crafting a lead-generating PDF.

The biggest mistakes people make are:

1. **Focusing on too many problems at once.** Sure, your clients have many problems they need solved, but if you try to solve more than one problem for them at a time, they may experience a little fatigue reading your PDF. Try focusing on one problem at a time.

2. **Using too much text.** Make sure to have the PDF laid out so the text flows and is easy to read. Make your PDFs scannable. Think about images, drop caps, callouts, and anything else that will move a reader through the document with ease. Less text is better!

3. **Being too vague.** This is not the time to get cute or clever with your language. If you are vague about what problem you're hoping your customers resolve, they'll be confused about what you offer. Don't say "The beauty of a canine companion," instead say "Three things to remember when selecting a puppy!"

4. **Not using a catchy title.** Make sure your title sounds interesting. If you'd never heard of your product or service, would you want to read an article titled "A study of market irregularities as it relates to home equity" or would you rather read "How to increase the value of your home in a down market"?

TEST YOUR METHODS
AND ADJUST AS NECESSARY

Test, test, and test again.

Once you put the lead generator on your page, make sure to track how it is working.

As long as it is working, keep using it. If it isn't working, take the time to create a new one and start all over. I'd say about 60 percent of the lead generators we've created have found an audience and 40 percent were duds.

Like I said, we built our entire early business on a PDF called "Five Things Your Website Should Include," but I was shocked that a seriously robust PDF called "How to Prepare Your Business for a Recession" got almost no response. I guess people don't want to think about a recession.

The most important thing is to have at least one lead generator that is working well for you and then to keep adding to it until you've got a pretty good number of emails coming in daily.

Once you create your first lead generator, you'll start collecting email addresses. Sadly, many people don't do anything with those email addresses. What an enormous missed opportunity.

This brings us to the fourth element of a sales funnel that works: email campaigns.

If you'd like to hire one of our StoryBrand certified guides to write a lead generator for you, visit our directory of guides at MarketingMadeSimple.com. Again, we do not participate financially in their business, but we did train them to create terrific lead generators!

7

THE POWER OF EMAIL

*How to Earn Space in
Somebody's Inbox*

What should you do once you get an email address?

The whole point of a lead generator is to get an email address. Remember, when potential customers gives you their email address you should consider them a hot lead.

Sending them regular, valuable emails is your best opportunity to continue building a relationship and selling them a product that will solve their problem.

While a few people will buy a product immediately, most will need to continue to learn more about your company before feeling a sense of trust.

Not following up with your customer after they download your PDF is like getting somebody's phone number after asking them out and then never calling them back.

If somebody gave you their email address, they are expecting you to email them. You got those digits, now follow through!

In this section of the book, we are going to guide you through two kinds of email campaigns you can send. Both will grow your company.

The two types of email campaigns we recommend are:

1. **Nurture campaigns.** These are designed to keep in touch with a potential customer and earn trust over time.
2. **Sales campaigns.** These are designed to close the sale.

IMPORTANT QUESTIONS ABOUT EMAIL CAMPAIGNS

We get lots of questions about emails from our clients. Most people are a little nervous about sending emails because it feels like they are broadcasting to the world. The truth is you aren't. You're simply broadcasting to a group of people who have asked you to keep in touch.

Emails are pretty hard to mess up. Nevertheless, let's cover some of the basics.

Question: How Many Emails Do I Send?

As many as you can while always adding value and staying interesting.

People often want to know what the "magic number" of emails is to send in an email sequence. But don't get so focused on the number of emails that you forget the purpose of the sequence is to keep customers engaged. We recommend sending at least one email per week. However, if you have something interesting to say, you can send with greater frequency. I have a personal nurturing campaign at BusinessMadeSimple.com that offers a free business tip every single weekday. Even though that may sound like a lot of emails, I've had tens of thousands of people subscribe and very few unsubscribes. I just make sure to keep the videos short, topical, helpful, and never boring!

Question: How Do We Master the Art of Writing Email Copy?

Learn from others and practice, practice, practice.

First of all, we have to remember it's not a mastery. You won't get it all at once, and that's okay. Just get a little bit better each day and you'll be on your way. In Chapter 10 I will walk you through some more in-depth practices for writing great emails, but if you have no idea where to start, here are a few tips:

1. *Read email subject lines you get from other companies.* Which ones get your attention and why did you open them?
2. *Read magazine headlines.* If you look at the magazines on the stand as you're checking out at the grocery store you will see what type of headlines get people's attention.
3. *Write in a conversational voice.* Write the way you talk, the way you would write to a friend or family member
4. *Always be thinking,* "What problems can I help my reader overcome, what value can I add, and what empathy and authority can I show to my potential customer?"

And the final four pieces of advice I'll just lift from Ernest Hemingway:

5. *Use short words.* By trying to sound smart and interesting, we often sound dumb and dull. There's no reason to use big words. While the written and spoken word are different, reading your email out loud is a great way to test whether or not it is clear. Using big words, insider language, and complicated phrases is a great way to confuse your customers. Never forget: if you confuse, you'll lose.

6. *Use short sentences.* When somebody clicks to open your email, they're certainly willing to give you a little more time than if they were browsing your website. But don't overdo it. Keep your sentences short so the email is easy to read. Long sentences require your reader to burn mental calories. At some point the reader will opt out if the calorie expenditure you're requiring is too great.

7. *Use short paragraphs.* When somebody clicks to open your email, make sure the text that unfolds doesn't look like a book. They didn't sign up to read Tolstoy. By breaking up the text into short, separated paragraphs the email looks like it will not take them much time and so they'll be more likely to read it.

8. *Use active language.* Active verbs make a sentence interesting. Instead of saying "we are having a sale" say "you're going to want to barge through our door because we've walked through the shop and lowered prices on most of our products." Words like "barge" and "walked" and "lowered" are interesting because they connote movement.

LET'S WRITE SOME EMAILS!

With those things in mind, let's look specifically at how to write both nurture campaigns and sales campaigns that your customers will actually want to receive.

8

NURTURE EMAIL CAMPAIGNS

Now Let's Nurture the Relationship!

What is a nurture email campaign?

Nurture emails are designed to be ongoing email campaigns that continue to "nurture" your relationship with a client.

Some people calls these *drip campaigns* because they slowly drip information to customers over a long period of time.

With a nurture campaign, you'll be dripping information to customers about how you can solve their problems and offer them value.

STAY IN THE GAME

The reason a nurture campaign is important is because most customers don't want to buy your product right away. Often, they have to hear about a product five or six times before they're willing to make a purchase. Why? Because they trust the familiar and don't trust the unfamiliar. And what makes something or somebody familiar? Hearing about them over and over from different outlets in different contexts.

So, imagine a customer hears about you from a friend. That's touchpoint one. Then they hear about you again from another friend. That's touchpoint two. Then they check out your website and because you used our framework, you invited them into a clear story and they have a much deeper understanding of how awesome your product is. That's touchpoint three. Then they download your PDF and that takes care of touchpoint four. Then they start getting emails from you, which represents, let's say, touchpoints five through seven. They discuss your product with a friend at work and that represents touchpoint eight. Then, that same weekend, they get another email from you, which represents touchpoint nine, and they realize they've been meaning to buy your product for a few weeks but just hasn't made the time. They finally sit down at the kitchen counter and pulls out a debit card to make that purchase.

That's how a relationship with customers tends to work. And because you're sending them emails, you sped up those touchpoints and entered into a relationship of trust much more quickly.

In fact, without those emails, they may have never placed an order at all!

PEOPLE BUY WHEN THEY ARE READY, BUT ONLY IF YOU ARE STILL AROUND

The truth is people buy when they're ready to purchase, not when you're ready to sell. It goes without saying, you are most likely to close the deal if you are around when they're ready to buy. Sending out a weekly email ensures that when they hit the buying window you, and not your competitor, are fresh in their minds.

Not only this, but by sending them a weekly email, you're showing up in the most intimate device they own: their phone.

Customers are walking around all day, staring at their phones. If you can send them a weekly email that reminds them you are a guide who can help them solve a problem, offer them assistance and support, and provide them with an immense amount of value for free, they are more likely to stay subscribed as you're communicating with them on the same device as their friends, family, and coworkers. Earning the right to be in that sacred space is critical. And it's an honor.

If you aren't leveraging the power of an email nurturing sequence, and your competitor is, they will beat you in the marketplace. It's absolutely essential that you are emailing your list consistently with valuable content.

NURTURE EMAILS ARE A GREAT WAY TO PLAY THE LONG GAME

By creating a nurture campaign you're committing to the long game.

Don't be discouraged. You could send nurture emails to a customer once a week for seven years before they make a purchase.

Stay connected until they want to make a purchase.

You may ask for the sale a number of times before they're ready, but if you're providing enough value in your nurture emails, they will stay subscribed even if they aren't interested in making a purchase right now.

Commitment in a relationship takes time. It's true in romance, friendship, business relationships—and especially in the relationships we build with our customers.

WHAT ABOUT UNSUBSCRIBES?

The unsubscribe button is your friend. You don't want to waste your customers' time and you don't want an email list full of people who don't want to receive them.

Because your customers can unsubscribe from your emails at any point, you don't have to feel guilty about bothering them. Everybody knows how to unsubscribe these days, so if they're not unsubscribing, they like you. And you should feel great about that.

You don't have to worry about them not opening your emails, either. There are plenty of companies whose nurture campaigns I subscribe to that I hardly open. But those emails are super powerful anyway. Why? Because once a week or more I am seeing the name of that company as I swipe and delete that email. It's fantastic branding. Even though they are sending me a bunch of emails I am not reading, because those emails come from them, I am being reminded that they exist. So when I am ready to actually buy a pair of shoes or a power tool or a vacation with my wife, I have a company fresh in my mind to call.

WHAT SHOULD AN EMAIL ACCOMPLISH?

Many, if not most, people will not open your emails—but a good percentage of people will. That means we need to write some really great emails.

Later I'll give you some formulas so that writing emails gets easier. And more fun. But for now here's a high-level overview of what emails should accomplish:

- ▸ **Solve a problem.** Never miss an opportunity to tell
  people why you matter. And why do you matter? Because

you solve a specific problem. Tell customers what that problem is and they will remember you forever.

▸ **Offer value.** What information, access, and tips can you offer your potential customers that help them get what they want?

▸ **Remind them you have a solution**. Don't mention a problem if you aren't going to position yourself as the one who resolves it. What products do you have that solve your customers' problems?

▸ **Send customers back to your website**. They came once, downloaded your lead magnet, and showed interest. Now it's time to bring them back with fresh eyes. Your website is the perfect elevator pitch: by bringing them back you get to make that pitch again.

Many of our clients feel timid about selling their products and services. They don't want to come off like infomercial pitchmen, emotionally strong-arming customers out of their money.

One great characteristic of an email nurturing campaign is that it offers free value. Of course you always want to mention that you have more products, but this is hardly strong-arm selling.

A nurturing campaign does something even more powerful than selling your product. It positions you as the forever guide your customer has been looking for. Really, the goal of a nurturing campaign is to make sure the customer knows that, in the area of your expertise, you're the first person they need to call.

This means all the information you give away should be your expert advice on what's going wrong in your customers' lives and how their lives can be made better.

If you sell athletic shoes, you can tell your customers why the shoes they used to wear don't last, why people have back pain, and how the right pair of shoes can turn them into an athlete.

If they want to take a deeper dive, they can purchase your shoes.

If you sell a management consulting services you can talk about why common management assumptions are wrong, about mistakes managers make, or about the need to set up an actual execution plan.

If they want to take a deeper dive, they can purchase your consulting.

You want to keep giving your customer information on *why* the way they are living their lives without your product is not working, all the while positioning your product as the *how* that will fix their problem.

THE STRUCTURE OF A BASIC NURTURE SEQUENCE

There are many ways you can nurture customers. For the purposes of allowing you to create an initial, effective campaign, I am going to walk you through three types of nurture sequences that are easy to create and will work right away.

Kinds of Email Nurturing Campaigns

Weekly announcements. Every Monday morning we send out a nurture email with a preview of our podcast. Our podcast delivers content from experts that will help companies grow, which means every week our entire list receives some kind of beneficial content.

The real power of the email podcast announcement is that it gives me an excuse to send an email to my list, week after week. And each email explains how we've interviewed an expert to deliver even more value.

Honestly, it's hard to know what is more valuable in terms of growing our business, the podcast or the email we send each week announcing each episode's guest. Both are terrific touchpoints for our customers.

What could you email your customers about each week? A weekly product focus? A Monday morning management tip? An educational series that will turn them into a great guitar player?

Find a reason to email your customers so you remind them you exist.

Even though the point of a nurture email is not to sell product, you should still include a mention of your product at the end of each email. This mention is not a hard sell, just a small reminder that lets customers know what you do and what products you create that may solve their problems.

In our weekly podcast announcements, we take it a step further. While the purpose of the email is to let people know about our podcast, we include an ad at the bottom of the email reminding subscribers about our products.

Here's a sample of one of those weekly emails:

Catchy Title:
Is the Financial System Ripping You Off?

Short Description of Content:
How much do financial markets actually impact your small business? More than you probably realize. And in this case, what you don't know really can hurt you—and your employees. Today on the podcast, Josh Robbins will arm you with the information you need to make smart decisions about your financial advisors, investments, and 401k plans—without getting taken advantage of.

Call to Action:
Listen now

Is the Financial System Ripping You Off?

How much do financial markets actually impact your small business? More than you probably realize. And in this case, what you don't know really can hurt you -- and your employees. Today on the podcast, Josh Robbins will arm you with the information you need to make smart decisions about your financial advisors, investments and 401k plans -- without getting taken advantage of.

LISTEN NOW

Short Ad:
Story Brand Live Marketing Workshop May 19–20

As more companies experience the power of the StoryBrand Framework, our marketing workshops get bigger and bigger. But this next one is a little different.

Our next workshop is happening May 19–21, at Clementine Hall in Nashville. Clementine Hall is a beautiful venue with a really intimate feel, and it's probably the last time we'll do a Live Marketing Workshop with this small of a group. Don't miss it!

Second Call to Action:
Register now

Share weekly tips. Another kind of weekly email you can send would be a collection of tips that will make your customers' lives better as it relates to your products and services.

You can offer something consistent every week, like a weekly cocktail or cooking recipe, or you can offer tips that help them organize their homes, their time, or their lives.

If you are having a hard time deciding what type of tips to send, survey your subscribers to see what kinds of content they want to receive. What do they need help with? What are the top three problems they encounter every week?

You can also look at your social media platforms and analyze which posts have the most interactions. Are there pictures or tips that your tribe is typically drawn to? Use those as launching points for creating new and helpful content.

If you are a store that sells cookware, your customer wants to be a great at-home chef, but they don't know the first thing about seasonings. Take them to seasonings school! Every week, send them a description of a feature seasoning. Tell them where to use each seasoning, where it came from, and why it's so wonderful to include in a dish. And for heaven's sake, include recipes. (If anybody creates this nurturing campaign, by the way, sign me up!)

Here are a few kinds of weekly tip emails that have been powerful for our clients:

- Weight loss tips
- Cocktail recipes
- Fashion tips
- Leadership tips
- Motivational Monday tips
- Weekly activities to do with your kids
- New yoga poses
- Tips on social media marketing
- Dog-training tips
- Tips on personal safety
- Each-week-of-the-year gardening projects
- A parent-to-adolescent language translator

There is no end to the list of what you can offer your customers. Remember, you're an expert and they want to know more. Step into your authority and teach them what you know!

The structure of these types of emails is fairly simple.

Think of the email as a blog post or short magazine article.

▶ **Start with a clear title.** This is not the time to be clever. The title can be catchy, but be very clear about what you've included inside the email. If I have to guess about the content, I'm not going to open the email.

▶ **State the problem.** Use a short description that addresses the customers' problem and lets them know you are going to reveal a solution.

▶ **Deliver the strategic tip or value.** Simply let them know how to solve their problem. Break the problem down into steps if you can. Remember, even emails should be visual.

▶ **Position yourself as the guide.** You position yourself as the guide by expressing empathy and demonstrating authority or competency. Make sure you have a short statement about how or why you care that your customers are struggling and then let them know why you are qualified to help.

▶ **Let them know you have a product to sell.** Finally, make sure to mention your product or service. You will get a few orders when you do this, but that's not the point. The point is to continue taking your potential customers through an exercise in memorization. You are teaching them to memorize what problems you solve and what products you sell.

Here is an example of a weekly tip email that works:

Clear Title:
Ten Tips for Losing Fifteen Pounds

We know that when it comes to losing that last fifteen pounds, the old rules no longer apply.

With the final fifteen, suddenly you're in a whole new universe.

Our doctors and researchers have discovered a reason and it's this: your set point has changed. What that means is that even though you've got fifteen pounds left to lose, your body thinks you are skinny!

But don't worry. We've helped thousands of people drop the final fifteen and we can help you too.

The key is to stay active and get serious. You're going to have to approach this like a baseball player approaches an opposing pitcher.

Get your strategy set, and you'll find success.

So without further delay, here are our top ten tips to losing the last fifteen pounds.

Ten Tips to Lose The Last Fifteen Pounds

1. Let those who are around you know what you're doing and find an accountability partner and/or group.

    We believe that when you surround yourself with like-minded, motivated individuals, you drastically increase your chances of succeeding. (We see it happen daily!)

2. Remove all unhealthy temptations from your cupboards, refrigerator, and pantry.

    Why have tempting foods in your house that don't align with your goals? Temptation removed = setbacks removed!

3. Create a specific shopping list based on healthy 400–600 calorie meals.

    Do not go into a grocery store blindly. Have a preplanned list and stick to the outside perimeter of the store where you will find whole, healthy food items. (P.S. Bonus tip: In addition to a list, give yourself a time limit so you're not tempted to browse. If you're a parent, your kids will love this game!)

4. Skip a few meals.

   If your doctor approves, feel free to skip breakfast, lunch, or dinner every once in a while. More and more studies are revealing that your intestines think a little break is actually good for you. It teaches you to live without food, stabilizes your blood sugar, and ignites your body to start burning fat. Plan to skip three or four meals each week and enjoy the break your body has really been hungry for. Want to know more? Google "intermittent fasting" and do some research for yourself.

5. Drink more water! You need to drink at least half of your body weight in ounces every single day.

   Find a water bottle that helps you track your ounces consumed per day. If you have a hard time remembering to drink water, set an alarm on your phone while you are working to develop this as a new habit.

6. Write down what you eat.

   Keep a calorie journal. But don't just keep a calorie journal to count calories, keep a journal to practice awareness. Most people forget nearly half of what they eat in a day. By writing down what you eat, you'll start to see patterns and trends you can improve on. Plus, who wants to write down that bowl of ice cream at the end of the day?

7. Increase the amount of protein you are eating daily. Look for products that contain undenatured whey protein.

   Your body doesn't store protein as quickly as it stores carbs. Plus, protein is the building block of lean muscle, which actually helps you burn more calories. Increase the amount of protein that you eat, then, and you'll be more likely to lose weight.

8. Stop your stress.

You're not imagining it when stress and weight gain seem to go hand in hand. Stress raises the levels of cortisol in your body, which makes your body store fat at a higher rate.

9. Drink whey protein right before your head hits the pillow at night.

When your body breaks down protein while you sleep, it also helps the release of stubborn belly fat. (You really can add to your results while you rest!)

10. Get adequate, uninterrupted sleep every night. Include a healthy dose of natural melatonin.

Sleep is essential to any healthy lifestyle. Your body requires a full seven to eight hours of rest per night. Sleeping any less, even if you don't "feel" tired, is stopping your body from performing at its best.

We know how hard it is to lose the final fifteen, but we also know it's possible. And it's not only possible, it's can also be fun.

We've helped 1,245 people lose fifteen pounds right here in our gym. That's because when you sign up for our biweekly workout class, we don't even have you lift a finger without sitting down and learning a little about how your body burns fat.

If you'd like to attend one class for free, just call us today. We'd be glad to help.

When it comes to losing the final fifteen (or the first twenty!) we just might be the people you've been looking for.

Call us right now and we'll book you in the next class.

Contact info: _____

Sincerely,
Jim Smith, Health and Wellness Gym

P.S. If you bring a friend, we'll give both of you the first two workouts for free! Call us today.

The great thing about this email is it offers to solve a problem whether the customer pays the gym anything or not. But it also offers to hold the customer's hand if they'd like to solve the problem together.

The chances of losing that final fifteen pounds would obviously increase dramatically with your help. Even if you think the information is obvious, your customer may be approaching their weight-loss journey for the first time, or need a reminder. This email would work to earn trust and increase customer engagement.

Another great thing about the content of this email is it could actually be turned into ten consecutive weekly emails. Take each tip and elaborate on it a little further and ten weeks' worth of terrific content are ready to go. That's ten touchpoints with a customer!

Share a weekly notification. Like you, I subscribe to many marketing emails from companies who have product I want to know about. While some of their emails may have helpful information, mostly I'm on their lists to see what new products they are developing or to be notified about special promotions.

If you have a brand that consistently makes or carries new products, your nurturing email can simply contain a catalog-style page revealing what's new. You don't have to overthink it.

That said, including the occasional email about how your products are made (always to solve a customer's problem) or tips for best uses of your products will add to the overall depth of your offering. And they will also add some personality to the brand.

A recent shoe brand I consulted with wanted to know the fastest way to increase revenue. They'd spent a great deal of effort and money on branding and had sent their customers' email after email talking about the mission of the company, but they'd failed to do the one thing that would grow their company the fastest: send emails with pictures of their shoes.

I recommended they split their list into four: women, men, teens, and parents of children and then send a weekly email featuring images of shoes that fit those specific demographics.

Another company I worked with in Fort Worth, Texas, grew their company by simply sending out pictures of trucks. They were (and are) the largest seller of used lift trucks in the world. What weekly notifications did we decide to send out? Truck Tuesday: a weekly email showing images of trucks recently added to their inventory. What truck guy wouldn't want to receive that email each week? I already have a truck and I still open every email.

The key to weekly notifications that feature products is to make sure you're always letting customers know about something that is new and exciting.

In these types of nurturing campaigns, of course, you'll want to include the "buy now" or "shop" direct calls to action next to the product.

Other types of weekly notifications emails that have been successful for our clients include:

- ▶ Calendar of events for the week
- ▶ Weekly specials for a restaurant
- ▶ New weekly inventory
- ▶ Plant of the week (for a nursery)
- ▶ New houses on the market in your neighborhood
- ▶ Stocks to watch
- ▶ Specials such as 10 percent off this week

▶ Weekly recipes
▶ Weekly how-to videos

One critical mistake we've seen a few companies make is to fill their nurture emails with information about them as a company. Hitting your list with weekly introductions to the different members of your staff doesn't solve your customers' problems, and they won't be interested.

Also, keep the email titles clear and consistent so people know not to miss what they are looking for.

START SLOW AND ENJOY THE PROCESS

The nice thing about your nurture campaign is it's all automated, and you don't have to add to it every week. Simply start by crafting a few great emails, and when you start seeing customer engagement increase, you'll be motivated to add a few more. Pretty soon you'll have fifty-two emails that are delivering value and earning trust.

If you haven't been sending consistent nurture emails and the idea of doing something every week feels overwhelming, don't worry. Start slow. Repurpose content you have already created. And if you aren't a writer, hire a writer to help you out. I like to think I'm a pretty good writer, but I hire copywriters all the time because I love seeing what they come up with, and I love sending out words from a fresh, fun new voice.

WHERE CAN I GET EMAIL IDEAS?

Once you realize how easy and fun it is to send emails, you'll start seeing opportunities all the time.

Many of you came up with five or ten PDF ideas, but you're only going to create one. What about using those other four or nine PDF titles and turning them into emails?

You can also ask customers what they would like to receive from you. Would a weekly recipe be helpful? A weekly workout motivation? Your customers may have some terrific ideas.

The bottom line is this: if you are not emailing your customers at least once each week, you're missing out. And worse than missing out, you're being forgotten.

You can grow your company the same way I convinced my wife to marry me. Just keep riding your bike by her house. Eventually, if you are helpful and nice and not scary, they just might marry you. Or, um, buy your product.

9

SALES EMAIL CAMPAIGNS

How to Close the Deal

While the nurture campaign is focused on adding value and building trust, the sales campaign will focus on closing the deal.

Creating an email sales campaign is your opportunity to share the full story of how your product is going to help solve your customers' problems and actually ask them to buy it.

An email sales campaign is not about being shy, it's about challenging your customers to take a step in solving their problems. Today.

GIVE THE CUSTOMER SOMETHING TO ACCEPT OR REJECT

The idea behind an email sales campaign is to give customers something to accept or reject. Remember, the relationship you have been cultivating all along is a friendly, kind, helpful *business* relationship. And business relationships are transactional.

If you fear asking people for money in exchange for your product or service, you *do not believe in your product or service*. You do not believe it will solve your customers' problems, resolve their pain, or improve their lives. If that's the case, find a new product. But if you truly have medicine that will take away people's pain or problem, sell it to them! It's the right thing to do.

Many people use passive-aggressive tactics to sell their products. They mention that they have products, but they never say "Why don't you pick one up today?" or "How many would you like to order?"

The customer translates passive-aggressive sales techniques as weak. It's not unlike back when I was dating. If I kept mentioning to a girl that she looked nice today or that I liked her taste in music or that we were reading the same book without, at some point saying, "can I take you on a date sometime. I'd love to keep talking," the relationship could have gotten creepy. People want to know what you want and where this relationship is going. People want something to accept or reject.

It's true that if you ask for a commitment too soon, it gets weird. But at this point in the relationship you've built with your customers, you can ask for a commitment. I give you permission.

NOT EVERYBODY IS WILLING TO COMMIT

Another thing to remember is that a sales campaign doesn't convert everybody. Most people will still not make a purchase. But that's okay. You've been respectful of their time and earned the right to be heard and nobody is going to fault you for asking for a commitment. By putting yourself out there and asking for the sale, you are going to be rejected quite a bit. But you are also going to be taken up on your offer. There is a name for businesspeople who fear rejection. We call them broke.

WHICH COMES FIRST, THE NURTURE CAMPAIGN OR THE SALES CAMPAIGN

We recommend starting with the sales campaign and letting it run for about a week. Then we want you to put people into your nurture campaign so you can stay in the relationship.

If you're wondering why we start with sales without earning the right to be heard, don't forget we've already earned that right with the one-liner, website, and lead generator. It's time to ask for the sale. And if the customer does not make a purchase, we will stay in the relationship with our nurture campaign, so they remember us when they're ready to make a commitment.

Often, we recommend creating the email nurturing sequence first and then inserting a sales email campaign later. Why? Because most companies will grow even if they don't have a sales email campaign. A nurture campaign is truly that powerful. But make no mistake, a sales email campaign works. We've seen customers doing terrific only with great websites, lead generators, and nurture campaigns double their sales once they inserted a sales campaign.

You are going to love this valuable tool.

Here are a few things to keep in mind when it comes to creating a sales campaign:

1. **Determine which product you're selling.** A sales campaign, unlike a nurture campaign, works best when it's focused on selling a single product. You can create multiple campaigns for multiple offerings, but don't confuse your customers by offering multiple products in the same campaign or by trying to sell multiple products at once.

2. **Identify the problem this product solves.** I know, I know. I keep saying this. But I keep saying it because so many people forget. If you were writing a screenplay, I'd bark the same reminder. Every story, every scene, every character only makes sense when there's a problem to be solved. The same goes for your sales campaign. Your sales campaign is not just selling a product: it's designed to solve a problem, and the product is the tool people are going to use to solve the problem. Your product gets to shine only if it helps the customer overcome a problem or defeat a villain. If you forget the problem, the product makes no sense. Decide what specific problem this sales campaign is going to help people solve and talk about it over and over and over and over again inside those emails.

3. **Turn the entire email into a call to action.** Nurture emails contain calls to action, and so they do a pretty good job selling. But sales emails are different. While a nurture email is trying to add value by solving a problem and then adding a call to action at the end, a sales email is going to make the call to action its primary focus. It's the point of the email. Every word, every sentence, and every paragraph must serve one purpose: to challenge customers to place an order. It is not good enough to ask them to place the order. In a sales context, polite requests sound weak and make you look like you don't really believe in your product. In a sales email, you are going to strongly encourage your customers to place an order.

4. **Give them a short window in which to buy.** You don't have to create a limited-time offer with every email, but if you can, you should. Tell the customer their opportunity to buy or to receive a bonus is going away. You'll notice in most movies the hero is up against a deadline. The fact of expiring time is forcing the action. If it works in movies, it will work in your marketing campaign. When clients

know they don't have forever to make a choice, they're more likely to act. Unlike a nurture sequence, you don't want your sales sequence to be long or open ended. Create a sense of urgency and you'll get better results.

LET'S CREATE THE CAMPAIGN

Writing a good sales sequence is more art than science, but there are formulas that will make your first attempt more successful. As you get better and better at creating sales emails, you'll be able to mix and match some of these ideas, but starting with a template or two won't hurt. I've been writing these emails on behalf of clients for a long, long time and sometimes I still come back to these formulas.

With that, here is an easy first sales sequence you can create:

- ▶ **Email #1: Deliver the asset ("here's how to use it").** Likely, your first email will deliver whatever content/lead generator you promised when they signed up with their email address. This email should be nice and short and shouldn't sell anything. Just deliver the free content you promised. The only thing you should add is your one-liner, so your potential customers are reminded, once again, why you exist and what problem you solve. After thanking them for downloading the asset and including your one-liner, let's give them a day or two to enjoy the read. We'll wake them up soon enough.
- ▶ **Email #2: Problem + solution.** In the second email, perhaps sent a few days later, you'll want to identify the problem you're going to solve for the customers. Once you identify the problem, acknowledge and empathize with

their pain. Then introduce your product or service as the solution that is going to resolve that exact pain point. While you'll definitely be selling the product at this point, don't expect them to place an order. Often it's the third, fourth, or fifth email that closes the deal. But in this email we're definitely letting them know we're going to pitch them. Don't forget, you want to give the customer something to accept or reject and that's what we're doing here.

- **Email #3: Customer testimonial.** If successful, your last email made your potential customers want what you're offering. But they don't want to make an impulse buy. One of the feelings they may have is that they're going to be played for a fool. Of course, we know they aren't, but we need to help them understand they're safe. One of the ways we feel safe is if there are more people involved. That's one of the reasons customer testimonials are so important. Find someone who has experienced success with your product or service, and capture that experience in writing. Remember to keep the testimonial short and full of soundbites. Don't let this email ramble. Often, this is the email in which you'll start seeing exciting results.
- **Email #4: Overcome an objection.** At this point many customers want to buy and maybe even know they are going to buy but have one doubt that is holding them back. In the fourth email, you want to help the customers overcome a common objection people have for not buying your product. And don't worry if you're not addressing whatever mysterious objections your email recipients may individually have. Your potential customers likely have an emotional objection, and by bringing up a similar objection, you'll give that emotion a focus. By helping them overcome that objection, you'll help them overcome their emotional resistance to buying your product.

▶ **Email #5: Paradigm shift.** A paradigm shift email is another way of overcoming a customer objection. Many customers will feel like they've already tried whatever it is you're selling. Comfortable yoga pants? Tried that. A housecleaning service that uses only organic cleaners? Did that. If customers feel that they've already used your product or service and it didn't work, you're done. They rightly will not place an order. But if you can explain to them how you're different and that they actually haven't tried something like this, exactly, they'll be more likely to look at you through fresh eyes. A paradigm shift is language that says, "You used to think this, but now you should think this way." It's a powerful tool used to make people reconsider buying your product.

▶ **Email #6: Sales email.** In this sixth email, only ask for the sale. You heard me right. Don't sell, just ask for the sale. At this point, we don't want your customer thinking about anything other than whether to accept or reject our offer. This is a great time to bring up the limited-time offer. Is an opportunity going to expire? Is the bonus that comes with the offer going to expire? If so, bring that up in the P.S. of this email and you'll have great success.

A sales email campaign is more art than science. There are a million kinds of sales emails you can create, but these individual emails, and this specific order of six emails, has worked for thousands of our clients.

10

HOW TO EXECUTE THE MARKETING MADE SIMPLE SALES FUNNEL

A Step-by-Step Guide

Now that you have all the individual tools for creating a sales funnel, you're going to want to create an execution strategy that ensures you will follow through and bring the sales funnel to life.

EXECUTION IS PARAMOUNT

Many people who read this book will feel like they've found hope. And I believe you have. But none of the feeling of hope amounts to anything without execution.

My friend Doug recently told his wife he intended to help out more around the house. His wife looked at him slyly and explained that intentions do not cook the rice. Doug got the point. Stop talking and do the work.

Remember at the beginning of this book when I mentioned JJ's dissertation? He proved that our messaging framework will help any business grow, but only to the degree that they actually execute the plan.

Having a strategy to execute your sales funnel will help insure it actually happens.

SCHEDULE SIX MEETINGS NOW
SO YOU WILL BE SURE FINISH LATER

In order to execute your sales funnel, you'll need to schedule six meetings. The people who need to attend these meetings will be web designers, copywriters, managers whose approvals will be needed, and any support staff who help these team members execute.

The reason you want to develop and execute your sales funnel through a series of strategically scheduled meetings is to create a system of objectives and scheduled accountability so that your team will produce a well-executed plan. All team members will understand their roles and tasks and be given deadlines to reach those benchmarks.

If you are creating a sales funnel on your own, stick with the meeting schedule anyway. Feel free to invite outside contractors. Outside contractors attending these meetings will help to ensure they understand expectations and will save you creative hours in the long run. If you are working with a StoryBrand Guide, your guide can work to schedule these meetings on your behalf and make sure you are in the room and contributing as the project moves forward.

Here are the six meetings you will want to schedule in advance:

1. Goal Meeting
2. BrandScript Script and One-Liner Meeting

3. Wireframe Website Meeting
4. Lead Generator and Email Sequence Meeting
5. Content Refinement Meeting
6. Results Analysis and Refinement Meeting

Meeting #1: Goal Meeting

The main objective of the first meeting is to decide which sales funnel to create first.

This may seem like an easy question to answer, but it will be more complicated than you previously thought. What are the objectives of the company? Is the company in a transition? Are we aiming purely for revenue growth or are we trying to grow a specific division?

When I conduct one-day marketing strategy sessions I start by trying to find out if the objective of the sales funnel we are creating is simply to increase revenue, or not. If the objective is to increase revenue and grow the company, my job is easy.

If the company leaders want to grow the company by increasing revenue, my second question is "What is the most profitable division or product that the company currently has on the market?"

The reason I ask this is because many leaders are so close to their products and services they can't see the obvious direction the company needs to go.

To understand how a business works, I normally think of it using the analogy of an old sailing ship. You know, one of those giant ships with twenty or more sails, all stacked on top of each other, billowing and propelling the ship forward.

By asking what the most profitable division or product is, I'm asking which sails are powering the ship forward. I also want to know what the least profitable (or successful) product or service is, and then I ask a series of questions to determine how much bandwidth is being spent on something that isn't working.

What Product Are We Going to Sell?

My theory on growing a company is to decrease the size of the sails that are not billowing and increase the size of the sails that are.

This differs from the way most business leaders approach their products and services. In order to grow their companies, most people ignore what's working and try to make something else start working too. But unless you have market dominance with the product that's working, the greatest opportunity is to pour gasoline on the fire that's already burning!

Regardless, the purpose of the goal meeting is to figure out exactly what we are going to sell.

After deciding what we are going to sell, we should set goals and expectations. We usually set goals by establishing three specific numbers. The first number is the actual goal, the second is a significantly lower number that represents a failure. By failure, I mean that if we sell only this few products, we need to analyze the product itself and then the sales campaign to see if the problem was with the product or if it was how we tried to sell it. The third goal is the fun one, and that's the stretch goal. If we hit the stretch goal, we know we're on to something.

Once you know what product you're going to sell and what your goals are, you can move on to clarifying your message around the product itself.

Meeting #2:
BrandScript Script and One-Liner Meeting

After you decide which sales funnels you want to create first, get started writing some of the content you'll use in the sales funnel itself.

In the first content meeting you are going to create your Brand-Script script and a one-liner. If you are not familiar with Brand-Script, use the free tool at MyBrandScript.com. Using this simple tool will help you come up with language you can use to populate your entire sales funnel. It will save you hours—if not days—off your workload and ensure the language you are using will engage customers.

The BrandScript and one-liner meeting should take between three and four hours.

After creating your BrandScript, transfer your answers to the BrandScript script. Another blank BrandScript script is printed below.

The purpose of the BrandScript script is to make sure you understand exactly what kind of story you are inviting people into. Once you define the story, you must stick with the script. Keep bringing up the same internal, external, and philosophical problems. Keep telling people what their lives will look like after their problem is solved. Continue to position yourself as the guide. Under no circumstance should you wander from the basic script—otherwise the story you are inviting people into will become confusing.

Here's a BrandScript script for your second meeting. You can also download new wireframes at www.MarketingMadeSimple.com for free.

At _____ [your company name] we know you are the kind of people who want to be _____ [aspirational identity]. In order to be that way, you need _____ [what your character wants]. The problem is _____ [external problem], which makes you feel _____ [internal problem]. We believe _____ [philosophical problem/statement]. We understand _____ [empathy]. That's why we _____ [authority]. Here's how it works _____ [plan: step one, step two, step three]. So _____ [call to action], so you can stop _____ [failure] and start _____ [success].

Once you have completed the script, read it out loud to make sure it makes sense and sounds natural.

Sometimes what looks good in writing doesn't sound good when spoken out loud. Use this opportunity to change some of the wording around so it sounds great.

This BrandScript script can now act as a filter for the rest of your content creation.

Meeting 2 Part 2: Create Your One-liner

Your one-liner is simply a truncated version of your BrandScript script. Use your BrandScript script as a filter to create your one-liner and the process will be fairly easy.

What problem are you going to focus on? What will be the result the customer will experience?

Take your time and make sure it sounds good and easy to repeat.

Ask these four questions to make sure your one-liner passes the StoryBrand test:

1. Does it sound normal when you say it out loud?
2. Is there anything that can be changed to make the one-liner sound more conversational?
3. Is it easy for your staff and customers to memorize?
4. Are all the parts simple but give enough info that nobody would need to ask the question "What does that mean?"

Your one-liner can be used in almost every piece of collateral you create for the campaign. It can even be used as the email signature in all of your nurture and sales emails. You can use it on your website or landing page, on brochures, on in-store signage, and more.

Not only this but your one-liner will serve as the controlling idea behind your entire campaign. If anything you write doesn't feel like it meshes with the one-liner, change it. Your customers will get confused if the story you are inviting them into is not consistent.

The final thing to do before leaving this second meeting is to decide who will be responsible for each task and what the deadlines are for each item.

Here is a sample agenda for Meeting #2:

1. Meeting opening:
    a. Introduce all those in the room to highlight that the reason they are there is because they bring something important to the table.
    b. Talk about the purpose for the day: to get everyone on the same page with a clear message about what the company does.
    c. Introduce the concept of BrandScript script and one-liner.
2. BrandScript script activity
    a. Introduction and purpose
    b. Group brainstorming
    c. Decision
3. One-liner activity
    a. Introduction and purpose
    b. Group brainstorming
    c. Decision
4. Assign tasks and deadlines
5. Remind people about the next meeting for website wireframe.

Meeting #3: Wireframe Website

At the beginning of the third meeting the room will feel different. Your team will be energized and focused and excited about the possibility this campaign will be a radical success. The group will also feel organized and on track, which will add to the excitement.

The objective of the third meeting is to wireframe the website or landing page.

The great thing about wireframing the website or landing page is it's also an exercise in memorializing your entire pitch.

The website will include nearly every talking point and will organize those talking points so they are clear and make sense to potential customers. Just as importantly, though, the pitch will start making sense to the members of your team. Don't be surprised if, during this exercise, people stand back and say, "Man, I'd buy this. This product looks really good!"

I can't tell you how many marketing strategy sessions I've done in which I had no interest in the product but by the time we finished wireframing the website found myself wanting to buy the very thing I was helping somebody else sell!

Wireframe the Website or Landing Page

Try not to have any agenda during this meeting other than to wireframe the website or landing page. Once you're done, call the meeting to an end. The reason you want to stay focused is your website will likely be the most important tool you create when it comes to closing sales. The emails will be important, of course, but every one of those emails will direct people back to this website. So don't get distracted.

The design team will ultimately help with colors, images, and the overall feel of the site, but your job in this meeting is to get the language and basic layout completed.

I usually wireframe the website on a whiteboard, asking everybody in the room to record our final decisions on their own paper wireframe. Why have everybody memorialize our decisions individually rather than just have one team member write it down?

Because by having everybody write down the words we've decided to use, you're getting the entire team, quite literally, on the same page. In their own handwriting.

Once I explain how we're going to go about the process, I start with the header, then move on to the stakes, value proposition, and so on.

As I mentioned in the chapter about wireframing websites, you don't have to follow the exact order I've created in this book. But the order I've put sections of the website in is great all the same. Feel free to improvise, but beware of getting too creative in your interpretation of what we've instructed. The word *creative* is often just confusion in disguise.

Remember the sections of the landing page from Chapter 5? You will use those to wireframe your page in this meeting:

- ▶ The Header
- ▶ The Stakes
- ▶ The Value Proposition
- ▶ The Guide
- ▶ The Plan
- ▶ The Explanatory Paragraph
- ▶ The Video (optional)
- ▶ Price Choices (optional)
- ▶ Junk Drawer

Feel free to use the chapter on wireframing a website in this book as a guide.

Also, have your BrandScript script and one-liner available to make sure you are using consistent language all the way through your landing page.

Ultimately, the third meeting should be a lot of fun. You should come in with some positive energy and leave with even more.

Here is a sample agenda to make this meeting simple, clear, and easy:

1. Meeting opening:
   a. Introduce all those in the room if necessary and explain why they are there and what they bring to the table.
   b. Talk about the purpose for the meeting: to create a website wireframe complete with all the sections of the website homepage.
   c. Introduce the sections of the website you will be covering today.
2. Review BrandScript script and one-liner and explain the website needs to stay on theme as much as possible.
3. Website copy creation
   a. The Header
      i. Does it answer the questions:
         What are you offering?
         How does it make our customers' lives better? Where can I buy it?
         How can they buy it?
      ii. Do the pictures you intend to use support the sales pitch or confuse customers about what you are selling?
   b. The Stakes
      i. What is life going to look like if the customer does not buy your product or service?
      ii. What negative experiences are you keeping your customers from having to deal with?
   c. The Value Proposition
      i. What positive results will a customer receive if they buy your product?
      ii. What does your customer's life look like if they buy your product or service?

    d. The Guide
       i. Empathy: what empathetic statement can you make that expresses your care, concern, or understanding about your customer's problem?
      ii. Authority: how can you reassure your customers you are competent to solve their problem?
     iii. Testimonials
     iv. Other: logos, statistics
    e. The Plan
       i. Three or four steps: What is the path a customer needs to take before or after buying your product?
      ii. What are the benefits of each of those steps?
    f. The Explanatory Paragraph
       i. Simply use your one-liner followed by your BrandScript script to make this section simple, clear, and easy.
    g. The Video (optional)
       i. Decide on video
      ii. Decide on title
    h. Price Choices (optional)
       i. How will you visually display the price or prices of this product.
    i. Junk Drawer
4. Assign tasks and deadlines.
5. Schedule or remind the team about the next meeting in which you will discuss email sequences.

■   ■   ■

Meeting #4:
Lead Generator and Email Sequence

For meeting four, you may not need the entire team. The task assigned in this meeting will mostly go to copywriters. Although photographers, designers, and whoever is handling your email marketing platform will also need to be kept in the loop.

The purpose of the fourth meeting is to decided what language will go into your lead generator and emails for your nurture and sales sequences.

The reason you want to address these pieces of collateral together is because some of the language you use will overlap.

By the end of this meeting, you want to have the title of your first lead generator, the basic content outline for the lead generator, a list of possible nurture emails, and a list of topics and types of sales emails you'll then ask copywriters to create.

Keep a list of all the lead generator and nurture email ideas you come up with in the meeting because any lead generator ideas you reject can be repurposed as nurture emails.

The first goal of the meeting is to decide on a lead generator. Don't let this conversation drag on and on. The key here is to agree that you've got a good one, quickly outline the content, assign the writing to a copywriter, and move on.

The second task is to either create a sales email sequence, a nurture email sequence, or both.

I recommend outlining the sales sequence first, but only if you can follow the sales sequence with at least six or seven nurturing emails. This insures that your potential customers don't just feel sold to and then dropped.

If you only have time or bandwidth to create eight or ten emails, start by creating a good nurturing sequence then come back later and create a sales sequence you insert between the lead generator and nurturing sequence.

The perfect campaign would include a great lead generator, followed by a sales sequence, followed by a very long nurturing sequence. You may not get all of that laid out in this meeting, but you can make some serious progress.

The only mistake you can make in this meeting is to close it out without making firm decisions the team can act on. This time should result in an actual lead generator that collects email addresses followed by emails that build trust with customers and begin to close sales.

If you have time, you can dive into writing some of the emails together, but be sure to turn whatever copy you come up with to the copywriter who will be responsible for putting the entire campaign together.

A graphic designer should also be in this meeting so you can discuss the images you will use in the lead generator along with the images you will use (if any) in the emails themselves.

Sample Agenda:

1. Meeting opening:
   a. Introduce all those in the room if necessary and explain what their role will be as it relates to the campaign.
   b. Talk about the purpose for the day: to decide on a lead generator, create content for the lead generator, and outline the various email campaigns you have decided to create.
   c. Introduce the concept of the lead generator, nurture emails, and sales emails.
2. Review BrandScript script and one-liner as an effort to stay consistent in your content.
3. Lead generator

    a. Brainstorm a list of ideas for lead generators.

    b. Decide on the first one to create.

    c. Create an outline for content.

    d. Save unused lead generator ideas for potential nurturing email content.

4. Nurture emails

    a. Brainstorm possible types

       i. Weekly Announcements

       ii. Weekly Tips

       iii. Weekly Notifications

    b. Make a decision and create subject lines and brief talking points for each. Your copywriter will love the head start this brainstorm delivers.

5. Sales emails (outline the contents of each type as you go)

    a. Title of Deliver the Asset Email

    b. Title of Problem + Solution Email

    c. Title of Testimonial Email

    d. Title of Overcome Objection Email

    e. Title of Paradigm Shift Email

    f. Title of Sales Email

6. Assign tasks and deadlines.

7. Discuss when the next meeting will take place. In the next meeting you will refine the content.

Meeting #5:
Content Refinement Meeting

During meeting five, the campaign finally comes together.

I recommend printing out a physical, designed copy of everything involved, from the one-liner to every email.

Use Post-it notes and tape to put physical pieces of paper on the wall so you can see the entire campaign visually.

Why physical paper? Because these campaigns live inside computer screens and from here on out you will never be able to see them at a glance.

Have a member of your team prepare the wall so you don't waste a lot of time figuring it out. Once everything is on the wall, hand out printed copies of just the emails so you can read through them together.

Think of this meeting as similar to the table reading of a movie or sitcom. Before shooting a movie, actors and directors often get together and read the script while sitting around a table.

The process of a table read reveals the highlights and flaws of the script. If you follow our instructions, you'll be shocked at how good your campaign is and how much you've accidentally left out.

At our last table reading, we realized we hardly talked about our customers' problems at all. What an enormous mistake!

We were able to fix that mistake by writing language that defined our customers' problems and then inserted that language into every single email.

This process is so important that sometimes I will take different colored Hi-Liters and highlight text to make sure we're encompassing all the elements of a good story. I may use green Hi-Liters to highlight all the benefits our customer will get and red Hi-Liters to highlight all of the problems or consequences our customers are struggling with.

Looking at your campaign visually, using color-coded sections, allows you to see if your campaign flows and is even in its execution.

During the last part of this meeting, you'll want to schedule when everything will be launched.

What day will the new website launch? How often will you send out the emails? Which email campaign will you run first?

Here is a sample agenda for meeting five:

1. Meeting opening:
   a. Talk about the purpose for the day: to go over all the collateral created in order to get ready for the launch and to set the calendar.
2. Review and edit one-liner.
3. Review and edit website.
4. Review and edit the lead generator.
5. Review and edit the nurture emails.
6. Review and edit the sales emails.
7. Decide when you are going to launch the campaign.
8. Assign tasks and deadlines.
9. Set date about one month after the campaign launches to review the campaign and make changes and improvements.

Meeting #6:
Results Analysis and Refinement Meeting

It is important to make sure the collateral you created is working. I know that sounds simple, but it is so easy to launch a campaign and just let it ride whether it works or not. Don't make this mistake. Even the greatest of results can and should be improved upon.

What parts of the campaign are working and what parts are not? What can and should be changed? Who will make those changes?

Questions to ask?

1. Does one email seem to be working more than the others?
2. Can we duplicate what is working in other emails by adding P.S.'s or similar language?
3. What are customers responding to in terms of our message?

4. What are customers not responding to in terms of our message?
5. Are our calls to action strong enough?
6. What is the most confusing aspect of our campaign and how can we fix it?

If you have data, review the data. What emails are being opened? What percentage of people who come to the landing page are making a purchase? What's the open rate for each email? (I love to replace the least-performing email with something completely new.)

The objective of this meeting is to refine, refine, refine.

Here is a sample agenda for the sixth meeting:

1. Explain the objective of this meeting is to refine a specific campaign.
2. Pass out the emails for the campaign.
3. Review the data. What's working and what isn't?
4. Revise, edit, or replace anything that is not working.
5. Discuss what is working and see if you can use some of the language in other places on the website or in the emails.
6. Assign the revisions to those who will be responsible to execute.

If you execute these six meetings, you should see very positive results. Most, if not all of the clients our guides have worked with have been blown away by how much these simple but clear campaigns have grown their businesses.

While creating a sales funnel takes creativity and hard work, it should not be hard. In fact, it should be fun.

Years ago I took up the hobby of fly fishing. I mostly fish to hang out with my buddies and the truth is I'm not very good, but I still love getting out on the rivers.

Every time I fish, I can't help thinking about marketing. As a fisherman, you're always asking yourself where the fish are eating and what they are eating.

If you approach each of the six execution meetings wondering the same thing, you're going to do just fine.

CONCLUSION

Imagine a year from now that you have created one or two sales funnels that will grow your business. What does your life look like? What does your revenue look like? And what does that revenue allow you to do?

If you follow the plan we've outlined in this book, you will see results.

While there are other aspects to marketing, these are the basics. This really is Marketing Made Simple and it will work for you.

INDEX

transactional business
relationships, 64
trust
with lead generators, 117
with nurture emails, 155
in relationship, 20–21

unsubscribes, 144

value
adding, with statements of
problem, 39–40
in emails, 145
free, 115–16, 145
lead generators as, 115–16
in testimonials, 87
in weekly tip emails, 151
value proposition, 57, 77–81
videos, 57, 105–7

webinars, 123
websites
mentioning, in emails, 145
purpose of, 55

wireframing of, 174–75
see also wireframed website
weekly announcements, 146–49
weekly notifications, 155–57
weekly tips, 149–55
wireframed website, 53–112
building effective, 111–12
explanatory paragraphs, 98–104
guides on, 82–92
headers, 58–69
junk drawer, 109–11
language used on, 53–54
plans on, 93–97
price choices on, 107–9
stakes discussed on, 70–76
value proposition on, 77–81
video, 105–7
wireframe process, 55–58
wireframe process, 55–58
Wireframe Website Meeting,
173–77
words, power of, 36
worksheets, 120–21
writing tips, 135, 139–40

ABOUT THE AUTHORS

Donald Miller is the CEO of Business Made Simple and creator of the StoryBrand Marketing Framework. Over ten thousand businesses have used his framework to clarify their marketing messages. He sends out a daily business tip to more than a hundred thousand business leaders at BusinessMadeSimple.com

Dr. J.J. Peterson serves as Chief of Teaching and Facilitation of StoryBrand, as well as cohost for chart-topping podcast *Building a StoryBrand* with Donald Miller. J.J. is a PhD in Communication and prior to joining StoryBrand spent the previous twenty years teaching and practicing communication in the entertainment industry and higher education.

BUSINESS MADE SIMPLE CAN HELP YOU DEVELOP YOURSELF AND YOUR ENTIRE TEAM

Want to become a StoryBrand marketing guide?

If you have experience as a marketing agent and want to use the StoryBrand Frameworks to get better results for your clients, take the first step to become a StoryBrand certified guide. You can apply at www.MarketingMadeSimple.com

Want to develop your team to be competent business professional?

Business Made Simple is an online learning platform that is disrupting the university system. You and your people do not have to go back to college to learn tangible skills that will grow a company. Visit www.BusinessMadeSimple.com today and develop yourself and your people for an incredibly low price.

Have one of
our certified
marketers
**create a sales
funnel for you.**